Infamous
CHESHIRE

Bob Burrows

First published in the United Kingdom in 2006 by
Sutton Publishing Limited · Phoenix Mill
Thrupp · Stroud · Gloucestershire · GL5 2BU

British Library Cataloguing in Publication Data
A catalogue record for this book is available from the British Library.

ISBN 0-7509-4425-0

Typeset in 10.5/13.5pt Sabon.
Typesetting and origination by
Sutton Publishing Limited.
Printed and bound in England by
J.H. Haynes & Co. Ltd, Sparkford.

CONTENTS

Acknowledgements and Sources   v

Introduction   1

1. Historically Infamous   5

2. Infamous Cheshire Places   21

3. Days of Infamy   39

4. Infamous Characters: Men   73

5. Infamous Characters: Women   90

6. Court Cases and Trials   101

7. Callous Beyond Belief   122

Index   137

To my Cheshire family: my wife Pat, our son Nik and his wife Lisa, our daughter Penny and her husband David Bates. Not forgetting the major influence in all our lives: our first grandchild, Emily Grace Burrows.

ACKNOWLEDGEMENTS
AND SOURCES

I am indebted to the following for their support and generosity in the compilation of this book: Congleton Museum; David Hearn of Crewe Library for his information on the Great Train Robbery; Macclesfield West Park Museum; Mr Methane on www.mrmethane.com; Nicola Priest, editor of the *Warrington Guardian*, for her recollections and photographs of the IRA attack on Warrington; Timothy and Elizabeth Richards of Gawsworth Hall; Mark Thomas of the Royal Society for the Protection of Birds; Warrington Library and Museum Archives Service.

In addition I would like to thank the following for generously supplying and permitting the use of photographs: Mike Boden, chief photographer, *Warrington Guardian*; British Library, *Derbyshire Evening Telegraph*; Eddie Fuller, photographer, *Warrington Guardian*; Joe Griffiths and John King of the Lymm Local History Society; Hadyn Iball, Chronicle Group Photographic; *Knutsford Guardian*; Manchester Evening News Photographic; Liz Pearce, Stockport Express Photographic; *Runcorn and Widnes Weekly*; Greg Smith, *Thameside Reporter*; Viscount Daventry of Arbury Hall, Warwickshire, and Brenda Newell, administrator.

I must also register my appreciation for the following excellent publications which served as points of reference on the many fascinating aspects of Cheshire life: Peter Bamford, *Cheshire Curiosities* (Dovecote Press); Norman Ellison, *The Wirral Peninsula* (London, Robert Hale); Steve Fielding, *Cheshire Murders Casebook* (Countryside Books); Lawrence Lever, *The Barlow Clowes Affair* (Macmillan); Jeffrey Pearson, *Cheshire Tales of Mystery and Murder* (Countryside Books); Raymond Richards, *The Manor of Gawsworth* (E.J. Morten Ltd); Carole Sexton, *Tales of Old Cheshire* (Countryside Books); John Stalker, *Stalker* (Harrap Publishers); David Woodley, *Knutsford Prison: The Inside Story* (Leonie Press); Derek Yarwood, *Outrages Fatal And Other* (Didsbury Press).

INTRODUCTION

Present-day Cheshire with a population of around 1 million covering 900 square miles is one of the smallest of Britain's forty-four counties. However, its contribution to the history of the British Isles, socially, culturally and historically, is outstanding.

Despite its size, Cheshire has for almost 2,000 years been at the heart of the history of the British Isles. The Romans, from about AD 71, following a full-scale occupation of the area much later regarded as Cheshire, recognised its value. Not only strategically when using Chester as the staging post and holding zone for the invasion and suppression of the Welsh tribes, but also for its much needed valuable salt deposits. Chester became a major commercial and military site and Roman artefacts can be found all over the county.

After the Romans left Britain there were centuries of fighting between the Mercians and the Welsh with both sides having successful incursions into each other's territory before retreating to the established frontier lines of Wat's Dyke. Proximity to the sea along the Wirral coastline was not only a tremendous asset to the county but was also a liability affording an ideal platform for the Norsemen and later the Irish Norsemen and the Vikings to invade by sea. The Danes also invaded the county and it was towards the end of the first millennium that the name of Cheshire was first used.

In 1066 the Normans conquered England and, after Hastings, moved north and laid waste many parts of Cheshire. It was perhaps this troubled first millennium with its many wars that established Cheshire's reputation for its fighting men. After all, it was the Cheshire archers who were the dominant force in the English armies fighting the Crusades and fighting the French.

This immensely rich period of history with many of the great characters of the time passing through the county has, I feel, contributed to the legacy which has left Cheshire so involved with the modern world.

In *Cheshire's Famous* (Derby, Breedon Books, 2004) I focused on the numerous people either born in the county or who had spent their creative or formative years in Cheshire and had gone on to make their mark nationally and internationally. Explorers, Everest conquerors, sixteen Victoria Cross winners, world champions, Olympic gold medallists, Oscar and Bafta winners, captains of England at cricket, soccer and rugby, Ryder cup golfers, Wimbledon winners, award-winning scientists, Nobel Prize winner, television household names, pop singers, opera singers, literary figures, songwriters, film producers, novelists, artists, sculptors, inventors, politicians and

The historic county
town of Chester.
(Bob Burrows)

businessmen – all have succeeded at the very highest level. It is an astonishing list of achievers across the disciplines of human endeavour.

To ensure that my focus was historically correct I ignored the loss of areas featured in the 1974 boundary changes to include old Cheshire, while recognising the transfer into Cheshire of the new communities, as they are, after all, like it or not, now part of Cheshire. During my research all over the county I came across a number of Cestrians whose contribution to our culture was not always beneficial or indeed desirable. I also discovered places where infamous deeds had occurred and some places and incidents that had attracted national and, in some cases, international headlines.

Several of the Cestrians featured in *Cheshire's Famous* are also featured in *Infamous Cheshire* with the emphasis, this time on their misdeeds. Once again I believe that the reader will be astonished at the way in which Cheshire and its citizens have been involved in so many high-profile events, infamous trials, court cases and tabloid incidents.

Every county sadly has its share of murders and Cheshire is no different. However, Cheshire is home to Britain's oldest-recorded murder, Britain's most prolific murderer, and may even have been host to the country's most notorious killer. In 1712 one of the most unusual events in British history took place in London. Two noblemen fought a duel to the death over lands in Gawsworth, Cheshire. The full story is featured in Chapter One.

In more modern times Cheshire citizens have been at the centre of several high-profile court cases, which have dominated the national press: Britain's greatest financial fraud; the Parliament cash-for-questions trial; Royal scandal trial which sensationally involved the Queen, Britain's most infamous police persecution of one of its own; the nanny murder trial in the USA; and a show-business trial with the most damning verdict ever delivered by a judge. A Cestrian even featured in Britain's greatest ever train robbery.

The county hit the headlines when subjected to an IRA attack, a plane crash in a town centre, the police shooting of an escaped serial killer, a prison rebellion, and when it was reported to have the most dangerous road in Britain.

A number of Cheshire women have also achieved a certain level of infamy. Without doubt Cheshire has produced an outstanding number of characters over the years whose antics and actions have amused, bemused, fascinated and at times disgusted or appalled the British public.

Many of the places mentioned in the book will be familiar to Cheshire people, as will the names of the 'infamous' Cestrians featured, many of whom are national figures. I am certain that the incidents recounted, some shocking, some amusing, will be of interest to all and each one made the national headlines.

1

HISTORICALLY INFAMOUS

Cheshire has a colourful past and, as detailed in my previous book *Cheshire's Famous*, many of its citizens featured very prominently in the history of the British Isles. For example, the reputation of the Cheshire archers was famous or infamous for several hundreds of years depending from which side you viewed their exploits. The French in particular would regard them as being infamous. They formed the personal bodyguard of several of the early kings and were feared, rightly so, by this country's enemies.

Cheshire archer. *(Bob Burrows)*

SIR ROBERT KNOLLYS

Geographically, Cheshire was strategically important between AD 800 and AD 1700 and the many internal wars and battles across the Channel, not to mention the Crusades, afforded great opportunities to soldiers and adventurers not only to establish a reputation, but also to accumulate great wealth.

One man who did just that and at the same time earned for himself an infamous legacy was Cheshire's Sir Robert Knollys, born around 1317. He was a professional soldier of great repute who was also a ruthless opportunist. His reputation as a knight ensured that he was involved in the French Wars during the period 1340–50. However, he was far from being the idealistic knight spawned by romantic images of historical legend. He could be likened to a typical Mafia-style gangster of more modern times. During his fighting career he sought every opportunity to feather his own nest and to look after his own interests. His activities ensured that he accumulated great wealth largely through murder, rape, hostage taking, pillage and extortion. At one time he controlled most of the French Loire Valley, which contained forty or more castles with small communities. Skilfully he protected his back by informing his king, Edward III, that the towns and castles which he had plundered and retained were at the King's disposal. Indeed, he did lend Edward money, secured against silver and jewellery. With the King 'in his pocket' Knollys continued to build his fortune secure in the knowledge that the King needed him to succeed to sustain his own finances.

In 1381, back in England, Knollys quelled the revolt led by Wat Tyler and again earned the gratitude of the King, which resulted in him receiving massive estates and further enhancing his power base. Infamous and highly successful, Sir Robert Knollys died *c.* 1407 and was believed to have been the richest man of his time. However, he left no issue to benefit from his ill-gotten gains.

DR RALPH SHAA

An infamous sermon given by Dr Ralph Shaa on 22 June 1483 was so outrageous for its time that it has achieved notoriety as one of the most shocking acts of betrayal in British history. Ralph Shaa was the brother of Stockport's Sir Edmund Shaa, the founder of Stockport Grammar School, and at the time one of the most powerful men in the country. The highly respected Cheshire family left an indelible mark on British history but sadly, the mark left by Ralph Shaa was not one of which the family could be proud.

At one time he was the chaplain to Edward IV and also to Richard III. However, during this piece of turbulent English history Richard III inspired, coerced or corrupted Ralph Shaa to deliver a sermon designed to discredit and belittle Edward IV and his family. Shaa delivered the obnoxious, fateful sermon at St Paul's Cross, denouncing Edward IV's right to rule and questioning his legitimacy and the validity of his marriage. He uttered the infamous statement, 'Bastards slips shall not take root'. The sermon was regarded by many as shameful, shocking and a betrayal of the family he had known so well. At the end of his preaching, his job presumably done, he was rushed away from the scene. He was seen as nothing more than a puppet of Richard III. A dishonest action by a man of the cloth who had betrayed his principles.

It is not reported whether he formally regretted his action but history tells us that after the sermon and the public reaction, Shaa seldom left his house and was rarely seen in public. Although the sermon assured him of a place in history, it also made life difficult to bear and, in 1484, within twelve months of his sermon, he died.

SIR WILLIAM BRERETON AND SIR PIERS LEIGH

Political intrigue and justice were rarely compatible in medieval England. Two famous Cheshire knights were victims of particularly cruel and rough summary justice. Their only crime was to be in the wrong place at the wrong time having befriended the wrong people.

Sir William Brereton of Malpas Hall, Shocklach, was infamously beheaded on the orders of Henry VIII. At the time Henry was seeking an excuse to rid himself of Anne Boleyn and was trying desperately to establish evidence of her infidelity. The unfortunate Sir William was arrested on highly spurious evidence. One source stated that Queen Anne Boleyn dropped her handkerchief from the royal stand at a tournament in 1536 and Sir William Brereton, in an act becoming of a chivalrous knight, retrieved it for her on the point of his lance. King Henry VIII was far from pleased and, after leaving the tournament in a fit of temper, had Brereton arrested and imprisoned in the Tower of London. His gentlemanly act perhaps gave Henry further fuel for his suspicions. Nevertheless, despite his continual denials that he had ever had an affair with the King's wife, Brereton was beheaded. Henry needed a scapegoat, Sir William was in the wrong place at the wrong time.

Sir Piers Leigh of Lyme had the misfortune to be a great friend of Richard II. Unfortunately for him Richard was unsuccessful in fighting off his enemy, Henry, Duke of Lancaster who took over his crown. Henry then set about removing potential threats, including Richard's friends. Sir Piers Leigh was captured and beheaded and his head placed on the end of a pike and displayed on the turrets of Chester Castle. The body was retained by Carmelite monks and 200 years later the remains were moved and buried at the parish church, Macclesfield.

Two highly respected men guilty only of friendship, paying the ultimate price for loyalty. Infamy indeed.

MARY FITTON

One of the most intriguing figures of Cestrian and English history that still arouses interest and debate is Mary Fitton, who was baptised at Gawsworth Hall near Macclesfield on 24 June 1578. Conjecture and speculation are still rife over the question of her being the 'dark lady' of Shakespeare's sonnet. Many experts have pored over historical documents and have examined Shakespeare's text ad nauseam, to elicit conclusive evidence of the identity of the dark lady.

Mary was the daughter of Sir Edward Fitton who owned the manor and estates of Gawsworth. He was highly influential at the court of Elizabeth I and through his contacts Mary became maid of honour to Elizabeth in about 1595. An old friend, Sir William Knollys, was in charge of the Queen's household and promised Sir Edward that he would protect and look after the young, innocent Mary. However, Mary, who was by all accounts vivacious, bright, feisty and flirtatious, proved to be far from the innocent little lamb that Sir William had at first supposed her to be.

Very soon, Sir William, a married man in his 50s, found himself bewitched, and fell in love with her. In his excellent book, *The Manor of Gawsworth*,

Mary Fitton, maid of honour to Elizabeth I and the subject of a court scandal. *(Viscount Daventry, Arbury Hall, Warwickshire)*

Gawsworth Hall, birthplace of Mary Fitton. *(Bob Burrows)*

Raymond Richards gives great insight into the court intrigues surrounding the conduct of Mary during her time there. Although Sir William Knollys was in love with her, she became the mistress of William Herbert, the Earl of Pembroke.

Mary's behaviour and character had made her the subject of much gossip at court and her attitude, hardly bothering to conduct the affair with discretion, created resentment. One court observer noted that when she was going to meet the Earl of Pembroke outside the court she would remove her head 'tire', tuck up her clothes and then don a large white cloak and stride confidently 'in the manner of a man', to meet her date. No shy, shrinking violet.

Her affair with Pembroke also of course upset Sir William Knollys who was by now infatuated with her. However, the storm clouds were gathering and, in January 1601, Mary became pregnant and the Earl of Pembroke admitted that the child was his. Despite the shame and the scandal he still refused to marry Mary and an angry Elizabeth I had them both incarcerated in the Tower. Later, Pembroke was committed to Fleet Prison and Mary was banished in disgrace and placed in the charge of Lady Hawkyns for her confinement.

The Fitton family was devastated by the disgrace upon the family name and Sir Edward, after Mary's child died at birth, secretly brought her home to Gawsworth. The depth of feeling and disgrace caused by Mary's infamous behaviour can be gauged from the pain expressed in a letter written by Mary's mother to her daughter Anne who lived in Arbury. It was Anne who agreed to have Mary live with her, perhaps in an attempt to remove some of the pressure which the family were feeling at Gawsworth. The anguished emotions are displayed like an exposed nerve. The mother tells Anne that she receives no joy in hearing about 'your little sister nor of that boy' (Mary's new boyfriend). She goes on to say agonisingly 'better if I had died with her in childbirth, it would have saved a great deal of sorrow and grief and her from shame and such shame as never had Cheshire woman, worse now than ever. Write no more to me of her.'

Clearly, Lady Fitton had a great sense of duty and responsibility and her reference to 'Cheshire woman' underlines the shame and hurt that she felt at being let down by her own daughter. Mary, it would appear, showed little sign of repentance or a change in her moral attitude. It is believed that she bore two illegitimate daughters to Sir Richard Leveson, a friend of her sister Anne.

In about 1606 she married Captain William Polewhele and bore him a son and daughter. After he died in 1610 she married Captain John Lougher and the marriage lasted until his death in 1635. Mary died in 1647, aged 69, and in her will asked to be buried in Gawsworth.

During her time in Elizabeth's court, Mary was regarded as a great beauty whose personality and vivacity lit up the court and brightened the lives of those around her. Many people were ensnared by her and fell in love with her. But was she Shakespeare's dark lady?

As outlined in *Cheshire's Famous*, Shakespeare had a number of strong connections with the county of Cheshire, but did he ever meet Mary Fitton or know of her?

There are two reasons which strongly indicate that he could have known her, apart from the common knowledge of her disgrace and banishment from the court.

A professional actor, a clown in Shakespeare's company of players, William Kemp wrote a piece dedicated to Mistress Fitton, royal maid. He called it 'Nine Dais Wonder'. It seems inconceivable that Shakespeare would not have known of a written work fashioned by one of his own players and not know the object of his affections. If Kemp knew her so well, surely at some stage Shakespeare must have seen her and been in her presence.

The second point is also beguiling. Shakespeare's sonnet refers to three 'Wills' in its opening lines: 'Whoever hath her wish, thou hast thy will and will to boot and will in overplus.'

Could he be referring to William Herbert, Earl of Pembroke, Sir William Knollys and of course himself, William Shakespeare?

This is of course pure speculation but intriguing. The compelling argument used by those who discount Mary as the dark lady is based on the description of her given by Shakespeare himself. In the sonnet he refers to the dark lady with the raven black eyes and black hair. History records Mary as being fair with brown hair and grey eyes. Nothing like the appearance of the dark lady. Could it be that Shakespeare deliberately used a description totally opposite to that of the lady that he desired in order to disguise his infatuation? After all it would be awkward for him also to write a eulogy to Mary, having been beaten to it by a colleague, William Kemp.

Whatever the truth, and historians continue to speculate and argue the case, Mary Fitton was famous and infamous in her time. Today her conduct would not be greeted with cries of outrage but her affair and the scandal at court would have made her a target of today's media.

Duelling Dukes

The small village of Gawsworth once again features spectacularly in English history. Not content with supplying the central figure in one of the great historical court scandals, Gawsworth also featured in the most infamous and notorious personal duel ever fought on English soil. The duel took place in London over the right of ownership of the lands and estates of the manor of Gawsworth.

A dispute over the ownership of the manor of Gawsworth Hall led to a notorious duel in the eighteenth century. *(Bob Burrows)*

Sir Edward Fitton II, the last Baron of Gawsworth, died in 1643 leaving no heirs to the estate. When his widow died the struggle for possession of the estate began in earnest between Sir Edward's four sisters. The Fittons and their cousins the Gerards started a dispute, which after almost seventy years finally erupted into a feud.

The struggle had all the components of a modern-day drama or soap: several lawsuits, forgery, periods of open hostility, divorce, plotting and seduction. The years of fighting and argument, the rancour and dispute finally came to an end on a cold, damp, early November morning in 1712 in the most hideous fashion.

The husbands of the two ladies who both claimed to be the rightful heir to the estate, the Duke of Hamilton and Lord Mohun, decided to settle the dispute once and for all. Together with their seconds they met in Hyde Park to fight an illegal duel. The Duke of Hamilton was attended by Colonel John Hamilton; Lord Mohun was seconded by Lieutenant-General George Maccartney. While the dispute between the main protagonists was over a long-standing question of honour, there was also bad blood from the past between the two seconds, which made for a potentially volatile situation.

According to eyewitness accounts of the time, all four men drew their swords at the same time. Hamilton threw off his cloak, Mohun took off his surcoat and they then saluted each other. As the duel commenced the two seconds, swords in hand, attacked each other, but very quickly ceased as the main fight became bloody and then fatal. Lord Mohun had a reputation for duelling and had twice been accused of murder but got away with it. However, this was to be his last duel. The men cut and thrust at each other and in a matter of minutes Mohun collapsed and died on the spot. Hamilton, although wounded, walked around for a while but his wounds were very serious and he died shortly after arriving home.

Some people alleged that Maccartney stabbed the Duke of Hamilton but this was never proven. The Duke did not accuse him and he was not held at the scene. Surgeons later confirmed that Hamilton had not been killed by Maccartney's sword. He was found to have four wounds but it was a severed artery in his right arm which proved to be fatal. Lord Mohun also had four wounds. One sword thrust had entered his right side and exited through his left, cutting a main artery, while another thrust had entered his groin. He was also found to have three fingers dangling by a thread on his right hand.

The illegal duel concerning two high-ranking men who had slain each other caused an outcry of massive proportions. Queen Anne had a high regard for the Duke of Hamilton but was livid at the contempt which both men had shown for the law. Shortly after the duel Maccartney left the country and the Queen issued a warrant for his arrest. In a proclamation on 2 November 1712 she denounced both men for defying the law by fighting an illegal duel. The verdict that they had murdered each other was duly announced and cited

An Excellent Ballad of the
Lord MOHUN *and Duke* HAMILTON.
With an Exact Account of their Melancholy Deaths.

COME all ye people far and near,
Of high and low degree;
Sad tidings I have brought you here,
And therefore mourn with me.

It was a sad unhappy chance,
It was, I need must say;
Two Nobles great, in passion bent,
Cast both their lives away.

The one Duke Hamilton by name,
The other brave Lord Mohun,
Renowned men of birth and fame,
But O they perish'd soon.

Great men have got great daring souls,
And vicious hearts likewise;
For from the glass and swimming bowls,
Great quarrels do arise.

Which often end with blood and death,
Ne'er to return again:

Life is but one short blast of breath,
Here's two great Nobles slain.

If men of honour did but know,
That death would part their fray
And lay their lofty heads full low,
'Till the great Judgment day.

They would their passions bridle sure,
And not admit such strife;
But each one thinks himself secure,
'Till he's bereav'd of life.

It was a sad and sudden fall,
From grandeur unto death;
That these two Nobles here did fall,
And lost their mortal breath.

It was a sad and sudden fate,
That did the Queen surprize;
She has lost two brave subjects great,
And they have lost their lives,

Which might have serv'd the government,
In many weighty things;
Which made them all with tears lament,
That wrath such ruin brings.

Alas! alas! I little thought
Upon the other day,
That blooming honour should be brought
So soon to beds of clay.

Instead of trumpets loud alarms,
In courtly form likewise;
In death's cold joys, and frozen arms,
This man of honour lies.

Great men will not submissive take
A quarrel from a friend,
But strait they will a challenge make,
And mortally attend.

For satisfaction all in vain,
They prize no less than life,

A ballad commemorates the deaths of the duelling dukes, Lord Mohun and the Duke of Hamilton. *(British Library)*

John Hamilton and George Maccartney for aiding and abetting them. Hamilton gave himself up and was acquitted of murder on 12 December 1712 at the Old Bailey. He was convicted of manslaughter and later released. Maccartney had a reward of £500 on his head and eventually returned to England after the death of Queen Anne. He offered himself for trial and on 13 June 1716 was also found guilty of manslaughter and later released.

Interestingly, his trial was presided over by Lord Chief Justice Parker who was born in Leek and later chose the title of Earl of Macclesfield. Parker had an illustrious career with rapid promotion from barrister, MP, Chief Justice, Baron, Lord High Chancellor and Earl before falling from grace. He was at one time incarcerated in the Tower, having been convicted himself for corruption.

Lord Mohun was buried in St Martin-in-the-Fields, ten days after his death on 25 November 1712. The Duke of Hamilton was first buried in the collegiate church at Hamilton before being moved to the family mausoleum in 1852. However, following problems with subsidence adjacent to the mausoleum, his body was once again moved and reburied in Bent cemetery. It was the most famous duel in British history and unfortunately there was no victor.

JUDGE JOHN BRADSHAW

A Cestrian about whom history has a mixed opinion is Lord President Judge John Bradshaw who was born in 1602 in Wibbersley Hall, Marple. Bradshaw was educated at Stockport Free School and King Edward's Grammar School, Macclesfield, and trained as an attorney in Congleton. He was called to the Bar at Gray's Inn in 1627 before returning to Congleton, where he lived in some style. He was appointed Mayor in 1637 and soon embarked on a meteoric rise as his talents and ambition were recognised. Attorney General for Cheshire and Flint, Judge High Sheriff of Lancashire, Chief Justice of Chester/North Wales, Sergeant at Arms by order of Parliament in 1648, President of Council of State, Chief Justice of Wales, Chancellor of Duchy of Lancaster and in 1654 Member of Parliament for Cheshire gave Bradshaw an enormous power base to pursue his ambitions.

However, it was as Lord President of Court, when he presided over the trial of King Charles I in 1649 which earned him a somewhat notorious place in history. Charles I was tried on a charge of treason and found guilty. The prosecution pushed hard and insisted that execution was the only fitting punishment. The court reluctantly (there were many who believed that Bradshaw thought that execution was too harsh) passed a sentence that Charles should be beheaded. Judge Bradshaw's signature and seal was the first of the fifty-nine required to authorise the execution, which was carried out on 30 January 1649. Whether Bradshaw, powerful as he was, could have prevented Charles's execution and commuted the sentence to life imprisonment is open to question. Cromwell was a powerful and persuasive man and not someone to cross.

It may have been a coincidence that in February 1649, just days after sealing King Charles's fate, Bradshaw was appointed President of Council of Staff, the highest office in the country. Cromwell, it appeared, had ensured that Judge Bradshaw was rewarded for his troubled conscience. The two men did not always see eye to eye and after a number of disagreements Cromwell eventually removed Bradshaw from his high office. Significantly, following Cromwell's death in 1659 Bradshaw was reinstated. However, he did not outlive Cromwell by very much and died of the plague also in 1659. His funeral was a spectacular affair of great pomp and circumstance and he had the great distinction of being buried at Westminster Abbey, a favour granted only to the rich and powerful.

This Cheshire-born man had become one of the most powerful men in the land and had left a fingerprint, however infamous, on British history. However, death was not the final flourish for Bradshaw. Following the Restoration, when King Charles II came to the throne, the feelings of many throughout the land were satisfied when the supporters of the King took their revenge for the execution of Charles I. In 1661 they disinterred the body of

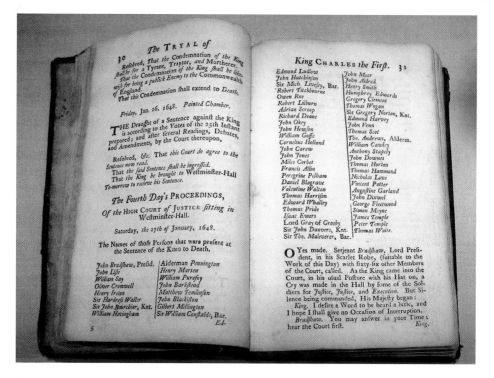

An account of the trial of Charles I, printed in 1737. John Bradshaw presided over the trial in 1649 which found the King guilty of treason and his name appears in the list of those present when sentence was passed. *(Both images: Congleton Museum)*

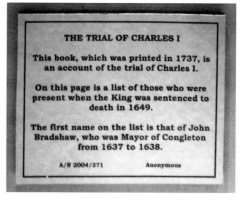

THE TRIAL OF CHARLES I

This book, which was printed in 1737, is an account of the trial of Charles I.

On this page is a list of those who were present when the King was sentenced to death in 1649.

The first name on the list is that of John Bradshaw, who was Mayor of Congleton from 1637 to 1638.

A/N 2004/371   Anonymous

Judge Bradshaw and hung it from the gallows at Tyburn. His head was put on display at Westminster Hall and the rest of his body was buried in a hole at the foot of the gallows. In a final act of revenge his vast estates and wealth were confiscated to prevent his friends and supporters from benefiting. Bradshaw will be forever remembered as the man who sealed Charles I's death sentence. Could he have prevented it? Did he really have the power? Wasn't Cromwell just too powerful to be disobeyed?

History tells us that Bradshaw was intelligent with strong opinions and not easily swayed; certainly he could not have held such a range of responsible positions without having remarkable skills. Clearly after the death of Charles he did frequently fall out with Cromwell and Cromwell took action against him. Why didn't he then stand up to him over the sentencing of Charles? Perhaps he did have the strength and courage to let his principles overcome his greed. If he did then he signed Charles I's death warrant knowing that he was to be rewarded by election to the office of President of Council. In other words he took the money, he took the bribe. Many have before him and many have since but his actions at that time in history have consigned the name of Judge Bradshaw to the infamous category.

FAMILIES AT WAR

War inevitably brings out the worst in people and many an atrocity has been perpetrated in support of a cause. Civil war, by its very nature where the fighting is conducted between people of the same culture, the same language, who are often fighting over the same piece of land, often features rough and summary justice.

The English Civil Wars of the seventeenth century were particularly hard on Cheshire with well-established historic families finding themselves suddenly on opposite sides after many years of living peacefully together and on many occasions gathering together to fight on foreign soil. Indeed several prominent families were split as they took opposite views. In the First Civil War of the 1640s, Chester was the Royalists' stronghold while Nantwich was the head-quarters for the Parliamentarians. Several actions were fought in the area and the church of St Mary, Nantwich, is said to contain in its grounds the bodies of hundreds killed in the Civil War.

However, there is one grave which represents the ultimate act of infamy: betrayal. Captain Thomas Steele was in command of the defence of Beeston Castle for the Parliamentarians when he was accused of surrendering the castle in the face of a Royalist attack. Tried and found guilty he was taken to Tynkers Croft, just behind Nantwich church, where he faced a two-man firing squad. He was shot in the throat and stomach, and his body was buried in the churchyard. Was his surrender an act of cowardice or good judgement in consideration of the saving of lives? Execution or murder? It is unlikely that the jury deliberated too long over their verdict.

Another interesting feature of the Civil War, which revealed the depth of passion created by fighting against an erstwhile neighbour, came from an entirely unexpected source. Lord Byron, a Royalist commander, was reported to have a female regiment fighting with him. Their fearsome reputation embodied a streak of cruelty which it was said often degenerated into bloody acts which belied their sex.

After one fierce engagement in 1644, Sir Thomas Fairfax discovered when rounding up the prisoners that the numbers captured included more than 120 females. Early assumptions that they must have been cooks or camp followers were put aside when they were searched. The women were each found to be carrying long knives and later enquiries revealed that they had been involved in the fighting and had used their weapons.

DUKE OF CUMBERLAND

The affluent town of Macclesfield has a permanent reminder of one of Britain's most infamous figures, the Duke of Cumberland. Cumberland stayed in Macclesfield in 1746 on his way north to fight Bonnie Prince Charlie (Prince Charles Edward Stuart). The decisive battle, which routed the Scots, was fought at Culloden on 16 April 1746. The battle was savage, with the Scots suffering more than 1,000 dead, but what made the action notorious was the fact that Cumberland had given orders before the battle not to spare the wounded. It is believed that many Scots were that day not only defeated in battle but were also murdered while helpless from their wounds. The action earned for Cumberland the nickname 'Butcher'. Macclesfield today has a Cumberland Street and a building, Cumberland House, where the 'Butcher' is believed to have stayed.

Cumberland House, Macclesfield, where the Duke of Cumberland stayed in 1746 before the Battle of Culloden. *(Bob Burrows)*

TRUMPET-MAJOR WILLIAM SMITH

Another Cheshire link with historic infamy is with the Charge of the Light Brigade at Balaklava in 1854 during the Crimean War. It was a Knutsford man, Trumpet-Major William Smith, who sounded the charge for the gallop into history for the 'Gallant 600'. Smith was born in 1822 and died in 1879 and is buried in the churchyard in Knutsford where his headstone can be clearly identified. He was not of course responsible for the decision to charge, but did sound the signal for the inglorious but failed charge into the valley and into the jaws of the Russian cannon.

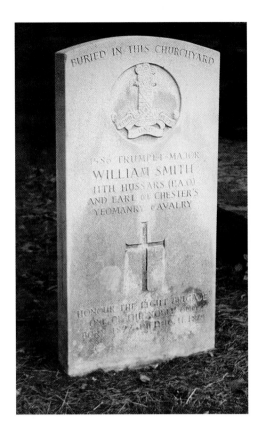

Headstone of Trumpet-Major William Smith, Knutsford. *(Bob Burrows)*

LADY HAMILTON

A Cheshire-born lady who would certainly dominate today's tabloid newspapers and be the darling of the media as much as she shocked English nineteenth-century society, was Amy Lyon. She was born in Swan Cottage in the tiny village of Ness, Wirral, on 26 April 1761. She never knew her blacksmith father who had died shortly before her birth. At about the age of 12 she moved with her mother to London and later worked as a maidservant in several houses. She became known as Emma and the world and history would eventually come to know and remember her as Lady Hamilton, the mistress of England's greatest sea hero, Admiral Horatio Lord Nelson.

Her early teens involved her in a number of sordid situations hardly befitting a lady who was to become the consort of a national hero. It is believed that as a 15-year-old she may have had experience as a prostitute. It is known that one of the houses in which she lived for a while was a high-class brothel. At the age of 16 she was taken as the mistress of Sir Harry Featherstonehaugh who found a place for her on his estate in Sussex. After a short period in Sussex, Sir Harry tired of his new toy and gave her, like a second-hand car, to a friend, Charles Greville, who found a place for her in

Edgware Road and paid all her living expenses on condition that she stayed faithful to him.

Despite his love for her Greville had financial difficulties and could not maintain the arrangement. He persuaded his uncle, Sir William Hamilton, to take Emma off his hands. Greville had to go to Scotland and suggested that while he was away Sir William take Emma and her mother to Naples with him, where he was to take up the post of British Minister. It was only after she had been in Naples for several weeks that Emma realised that once again she had been passed around like second-hand goods and was understandably distraught.

Soon, however, she was seduced by the charms of Naples. The villa, overlooking the bay, Sir William's attentions, visits to the theatre, sailing and being asked to pose by a number of celebrated local artists, ensured that she adapted to her new life. Adapt she certainly did. She was young, vivacious, dark and beautiful, with a perfect figure, and soon became popular with everyone, including the King and Queen of Naples. She was by now Sir William's mistress and he used his connections to see that she had music lessons and encouraged her to sing. It was during a visit to London in 1791 that Sir William, aged 60, married Emma, aged 26.

Emma had developed and matured and on their return to Naples she was able to take her place in the social whirl required of her husband's position. She could sing, act, speak Italian and was able to win over whomsoever she met. She was now a confident, outgoing young lady, a far cry from the gauche, 15-year-old housemaid/prostitute of just a few years ago. But her early infamy would pale into insignificance when in just a few short years her carefree lifestyle would be shattered, with the arrival in 1798 of Admiral Lord Nelson who sailed into Naples after his magnificent victory over the French in the Battle of the Nile.

Emma was certainly impressed by Nelson whose reputation was well known and she made no secret of her admiration for him. He in turn was captivated by her vivacity and very soon became besotted by her. There are confusing and conflicting accounts. When Nelson met her in 1798 some accounts said she was very beautiful 'of face' and others state that she was immensely fat. Reports of her being charming, vivacious and an excellent hostess are also in conflict with the opinion of a young English aristocrat who stated that, 'without exception she was the most coarse, ill-mannered, disagreeable woman that I have ever met'. Perhaps she was to him. But clearly she did not beguile him. Whatever her demeanour, Nelson was enthralled by her and made little effort to disguise his feelings for her. The affair became obvious to all despite the fact that Nelson and Emma were still married and living with their respective partners.

In January 1801 Lady Hamilton gave birth to twin daughters by Lord Nelson. Her decision to give away one of her daughters, leaving Nelson with the impression that she had only given birth to one, perhaps gives an insight into her true nature. As a teenager she had been passed from pillar to post like a piece of merchandise, with scant regard for her feelings. This lack of consideration shown to her probably contributed to her making such a selfish, cold-blooded decision. She is believed to have stated that she gave one child away because she thought that she would be unable to cope with twins. When one considers that she lived in the lap of luxury with servants attending to her every whim, her decision seems not only selfish, but also callous. Even more callous and calculating was the way in which she totally deceived the man she claimed to love, Nelson. There was also the small matter of a husband with whom she still lived. The retained baby was called, appropriately enough, Horatia, and Nelson was delighted, blissfully unaware of Emma's duplicity. They (Sir William, Emma, Nelson and Horatia) all lived together in a large country house, Menton Place in Surrey, after returning from Naples.

Fanny Nisbet, Nelson's loyal wife of many years, never stopped loving him, despite the social scandal and the humiliation which she felt at being so publicly wronged. Nelson ignored her protestations of love and carried on with his life as though she did not exist.

In 1803 the very strange living arrangements of the *ménage à trois* came to an abrupt end when the 72-year-old Sir William Hamilton died in Emma's arms. Nelson was also present and it is said he held the hand of Sir William as he died.

The affair had scandalised English society but it appeared that Sir William and Nelson had a respect and liking for each other throughout their strange relationship.

Less than two years later Nelson was killed at the Battle of Trafalgar in 1805. It was the beginning of the end for Emma. She never got over the shock and many of her friends deserted her. Financially she was initially comfortably off and wanted for nothing. Sir William and Lord Nelson both left her money in their wills and Nelson also left her the country house, Menton Place. But she had been used to being looked after since the age of 16 and had never come to terms with financial management. Her extravagant lifestyle continued and very soon she found herself in financial difficulties and had to sell Menton Place. Her decline accelerated and in 1813 she was imprisoned for out-standing, unpaid debts. After her release, heavy drinking exacerbated her depression and in 1814 she decided to escape from her creditors and moved to Calais with her 13-year-old daughter, Horatia.

Emma's attempts at a new start tragically ended in January 1815 when, after only a few months in Calais, she died at the age of 50 in their lodgings. From her humble background and early, sordid life, Emma became one of the most infamous and, strangely, one of the most romantic women in British history. Over the years her love affair with Nelson has spawned many books, television dramas and films and their story will continue to fascinate.

What of Horatia, their daughter? She married a vicar in Kent and their marriage was blessed with nine children. She died at the ripe old age of 80.

2

INFAMOUS CHESHIRE PLACES

For those who believe that law and order can only be enforced by draconian measures and that severe punishment acts as a deterrent, a glimpse into the past soon dispels this idea.

Over the centuries Cheshire, like every other county in the British Isles, went through periods of lawlessness when even the most severe punishments failed to halt the rise in crime. Theft, house breaking, assault and poaching were punishable by death or deportation. Beggars, common thieves, adulterers, even gossipmongers were placed in stocks, whipping stocks, ducking stools and iron jackets. The Cheshire village of Lymm still has a particularly good example of the early stocks, although of course they have not been used for many years.

Stocks in the centre of Lymm village. *(Bob Burrows)*

CAPITAL PUNISHMENT

In the early seventeenth century every Cheshire township had to have, by order, a whipping stock. Unpaid parish constables were charged with enforcing the law and as part of their duties, for example, had to ensure that no paupers or beggars from other communities entered their township to become a nuisance. Although there was no official police force until the early nineteenth century, there was a justices system dating back to Saxon times and enforced by the courts established by the Norman earls. Various stages of enforcement included the participation by powerful wealthy families, a later sheriff system with appointed officials and the parish constables who were unpaid elected householders. However, in some circumstances, such as civil unrest, including protests against unfair taxes, unemployment, food shortages and religious disturbances, mob rule and riots, the local militia would step in.

Incitement to create religious unrest was punished in the most barbaric fashion throughout the country. Cheshire has a monument to one particularly infamous execution, which occurred in 1554. George Marsh, a zealous, volatile, Protestant minister, had been continually warned against speaking out against Catholicism in a manner which was designed to inflame and cause antagonism. The authorities were forced to arrest him, and after being imprisoned in Lancaster, he was transferred to Chester where he was charged with heresy.

Undeterred, Marsh continued with his campaign and showered insults on the Bishop of Chester. After many unsuccessful weeks of argument and discussion in an attempt to get Marsh to recant or at least tone down his inflammatory rhetoric, the Bishop sentenced Marsh to death. On an April day in 1554 he was taken to Gallows Hill, Boughton, where, clutching his Bible and attempting to preach to the spectators, he was burnt to death. His remains were buried in the cemetery at Spital Boughton and in later years a monument was erected at the site of his execution overlooking the River Dee.

Women were not spared the agony of burning and, in the late sixteenth century, Boughton witnessed the burning of a woman who had murdered her husband. Pressing was a particularly brutal and premeditated form of execution designed to create many hours of suffering and there are several written reports of such executions in Cheshire. The victim would typically be stripped naked and laid upon his back while increasingly heavy weights were placed on his chest until many hours later he suffocated to death.

In 1656 Boughton was also the site of a number of executions of women who had been convicted and hanged for witchcraft. Hanging was the punishment for a whole range of crimes, including highway robbery, but there was an embellishment to even this gruesome final retribution. Murderers in the seventeenth century were hanged and then gibbeted. A gibbet is a metal cage in which the hanged body was placed and then the cage was raised by a chain to a prominent position high up on the scaffold to ensure that it could

Right and below: Monument and inscription in memory of George Marsh, who was burnt to death on this site at Boughton in April 1554. *(Bob Burrows)*

be seen. The rotting, decaying body which would invariably have its eyes plucked out by birds was usually displayed at a crossroads or other suitably prominent site to act as a warning to the living as well as to humiliate the victim, destroying his dignity and denying him a Christian burial. This barbaric punishment sadly did not always deter would-be criminals. Of the many gibbets scattered throughout the Cheshire county, there was one on the Chester–Warrington road, another at Trafford Green and one at Gun Hill, close to Meerbrook village, near Macclesfield. It is believed that the last time a gibbet was used at Gun Hill was in 1731. A farm labourer, John Naden, was found guilty of the murder of his employer and in front of a large crowd was hanged and then gibbeted.

A later record, in 1750, tells of a gibbet being used just outside Chester on the route to Parkgate. Typically for the time it was justified for the crime of murder. Four Irish labourers were walking from Chester to Parkgate when for some unknown reason (presumably robbery) three of them turned on the eldest, Bryan Malloy, and attacked him. After severely beating him with their staffs, one cut his throat with a reaping hook. They then threw his body into a nearby ditch after taking his money and some clothes that he had been carrying. However, unbeknown to the murderers, their callous deed had been witnessed by a man working in the fields. He had heard Malloy's shouts for help and had arrived on the scene but hid, afraid to intervene. He raised the alarm and the three men were later apprehended and kept in a barn overnight before being taken to Chester Castle, the county gaol. One of the men turned King's evidence and was spared; the other two were hanged at Boughton on 22 September. Later that night their bodies were hung in chains near Two Mills on the heath not far from Parkgate. The site is near Great Saughall, close to Chester, and now features a private house called Gibbet Windmill. It is believed that this modern house with its fixed replica sails was built in 1960 on the site of the original windmill constructed in 1773. There are several gibbets still surviving in museums and one can be seen in the excellent Warrington Museum. Mercifully, the practice of gibbeting ceased in the early nineteenth century.

In the eighteenth and nineteenth centuries public hangings were carried out at Boughton and in later years at Northgate Gaol. The last hanging in Chester was in 1883 when Patrick Carey was sentenced to death for a Congleton murder. Public hangings were regarded almost as a form of entertainment. Whole families would arrive early for the spectacle, bringing food and drink and jockeying for a good position. Musicians, jesters and jugglers would entertain the crowds as they patiently waited for the spectacle to unfold. It took a particularly unpleasant and gruesome public hanging to fuel the demand for public hangings to be banned.

On 9 May 1801 large crowds gathered at Gallows Hill, Chester. Despite torrential rain they were not to be cheated out of their entertainment. Three

Gibbets such as this were in use until the early nineteenth century. *(Warrington Museum)*

men were about to be hanged. Two of the guilty the crowds had little sympathy for as they were convicted forgers and had cheated and ruined the lives of a number of local people. However, the third, a young man named John Clare, had been found guilty of a minor burglary and the crowd had considerable sympathy for him. He had shouted out at his trial that he would never hang.

The crowd waited patiently and soon the cart carrying the men with their hands tied and their legs in chains made its way to Gallows Hill (now Barrel-Well Hill). As the sheriff's men helped the men out of the cart Clare suddenly threw off his ropes and made a mad dash through the crowd. The crowd fell back in surprise as Clare slipped in the mud and rolled down the bank of the River Dee. Soon they started to chase him, which also impeded the sheriff's men from trying to pursue him. The by now desperate Clare jumped into the swollen, fast-flowing river intending to swim across to the far bank and safety. Sadly for him the heavy leg chains pulled him down and he drowned.

'Scolds bridge', a gag made of iron which was clamped across the mouth. *(Congleton Museum)*

Ball and chain leg irons used for fettering prisoners. *(Warrington Museum)*

His prophecy that he would 'never hang' had proven to be true. Or had it? The authorities took almost an hour to recover his body. Then to the shock and horror of the waiting and watching crowds they dragged the wet, lifeless body of the hapless John Clare back to the gallows and hanged him from the scaffold.

It must also be noted that the two by now totally horrified forgers had had to watch the entire spectacle unfold while they waited for their turn to die. Any lingering hopes of mercy were quickly dashed and they too were duly hanged. It was also recorded that a final horror was inflicted when the cart carrying the bodies back to prison for burial overturned on the wet, muddy terrain throwing the still-warm bodies of the forgers and the bedraggled body of John Clare out into the street. It was the last public hanging in Chester.

Following on from Chester, Knutsford started to carry out hangings in 1886. Chester became a military prison. The Sessions House, County Gaol, would fly a black flag from the building on the day that an execution was taking place. Knutsford had its last hanging for murder in 1912. Cheshire has the infamous distinction of being the last county in Britain for hanging a man for a crime other than murder. Martin Doyle was convicted of attempted murder and hanged in 1861.

Despite the savage penalties, sometimes the harsh conditions of life forced people to commit desperate crimes. A case typical of the time was the attack on farmer Porter at Pulford in the summer of 1751. Porter employed Irish labourers to help get in the harvest. One night five of the men broke into the farmhouse, tied up and started to torture Porter and his wife. One of their daughters rushed into the room and, begging the robbers to spare her parents, told them where some of the family's valuables were. In the meantime another daughter jumped on a horse and galloped to fetch her brothers. Armed with knives and axes the men returned to the farmhouse, killed a man on guard and burst into the main room. Their father was naked and being tortured by the group. In the ensuing fight one of the gang was knocked unconscious and the other three quickly fled.

Two of the men were later caught on Chester Bridge and the leader was caught on board a ship in Liverpool. All four men were tried for robbery and assault, convicted and sentenced to death. The youngest of the group later had his sentence commuted to transportation and Stanley, the leader of the gang, escaped on the eve of his execution. The other two, M'canelly and Morgan, were both hanged. Harsh times, rough justice.

These days, rather than being regarded as a place of punishment, prison is seen as a place where people are sent as a form of punishment. Old prisons such as Northgate Gaol were clearly horrific places where incarceration was a punishment in itself. The conditions were typical of prisons of the time: cold, dank, dark, with no ventilation. Prisoners were kept in cells in the bowels of the building and one cell was called 'Dead Man's

Dungeon' where those sentenced to death were kept in terrible conditions before departing this life. Damp, with water running down the walls, and infested with rats and fleas, it was a daunting place. One cell hewn from under the ground was so tiny that it could barely accommodate one body. Indeed, one large man was crammed into this cell by gaolers who literally had to push him into the hole. It is said that he survived for almost two months before dying.

When the title of County Gaol was bestowed upon Knutsford in 1886, conditions had improved considerably. Prisoners were so numerous in 1811 that it was decided that a new purpose-built building was required to solve the problem. Work commenced in 1817 and when finished it was said to be a magnificent building – far too good for criminals.

The Sessions House at Knutsford became a House of Correction in 1860 and held about 270 prisoners, although it had been designed to accommodate 700. There was also a female wing that could hold up to 100 prisoners. However, although the food was considered to be very acceptable, the intention was not to offer an easy life to the detained. Physical tasks were enforced, such as operating a crank solely because of the exertion required, or performing on a treadmill and shifting heavy cannonballs from one place to another. Resistance was overcome by flogging, so although the conditions were generally more acceptable, discipline was still enforced.

From 1886 until 1915 Knutsford County Gaol carried out nine executions before it was taken over by the Home Office and used in the First World War as an Army detention centre. Sadly this superb building was demolished in 1934 and the site is today occupied by Booth's Supermarket.

CHESHIRE'S PRISONS

Today Cheshire has two major centres of detention for criminals: Her Majesty's Prison at Risley, Warrington, and Her Majesty's Women's Prison at Styal, Wilmslow.

Risley was opened in May 1965 as a remand centre and after the women were transferred to Styal Prison in 1999 it became a Category C prison. Today, with more than 1,100 inmates, it is the largest Category C prison – that is, a secure prison for those considered unlikely to abscond – in the country.

It has had a chequered history and one account of life inside, in about the early 1980s, is damning. A former prisoner wrote that conditions were horrendous for everyone in the prison, including inmates, staff, women and young offenders. He stated that the food was 'pig swill', brutality was rife, hygiene non-existent, the cells were too small, the bedding soiled and the use of the liquid cosh rampant, all of which made for a grim existence.

HM Prison, Risley, near Warrington, the scene of an uprising in 1989. *(Bob Burrows)*

In 1988, following a visit to Risley, the Chief Inspector of Prisons gave a damning report on the conditions there which seemed to confirm the prisoner's account. He described Risley as 'dirty, dilapidated, squalid, barbarous and appalling'. He went on to state that conditions were unacceptable and improvements were urgently needed. The prison had been built in 1965 to accommodate 608 male and female prisoners. By the mid-1980s it was holding 956 prisoners. Not only was the food appalling but also prisoners were confined to their cells for twenty hours a day. A spate of suicides underlined the pressure-cooker situation that was coming to the boil.

On 1 May 1989 unrest manifested itself in a headline-making prisoners' rebellion. More than 100 prisoners from D wing decided to stage a protest. The riot police, armed with shields and staves moved in. Quickly, fighting erupted, doors were torn off hinges to use as barricades and the inmates gained control of D wing and its flat roof.

For three days more than fifty protestors stood on the roof holding banners and informing the media of the terrible conditions in the prison and demanding an official inquiry.

It is said that some prison officers shouted racial taunts at the prisoners in order to split their ranks: 'Throw the niggers off the roof', etc. After the three days they surrendered, having ensured that they were photographed in case they were subjected to violent reprisals.

In 1990 the ringleaders, twenty-one men, stood trial charged with riot and criminal damage. The men protested that the prison conditions were appalling and that that was the sole reason for their protest. The judge would not accept their reasoning and directed the jury to ignore their arguments but the jury had been shocked to hear their stories and all the men were acquitted.

The riot which was followed a year later by an uprising at Strangeways was a watershed in the British prison system. The government were taken to task by the media and for a time conditions improved. The severe damage committed during the uprising led to considerable rebuilding at Risley and the men's remand centre was converted to category C, accommodating prisoners serving medium-length sentences.

However, conditions in the women's wings at Risley in the 1990s were far from satisfactory and the Chief Inspector was told of overcrowding, appalling food, bug infestation, unsanitary conditions and inmates locked in their cells all day, released only for meals. In 1996 and 1997 two young women, who were non-violent offenders, hanged themselves in their cells. In 1999 the 159 female prisoners were transferred to Styal Women's Prison, the second largest women's prison in the country.

Opened in 1963, Styal, a semi-secure prison for women serving short sentences to life, has more than 400 inmates. Proposals to almost double the

HM Prison, Styal, the second-largest prison for women in Britain. *(Bob Burrows)*

Entrance to HM Prison, Styal. The prison was the subject of a fly-on-the-wall documentary in 1981. *(Bob Burrows)*

capacity to make it the largest women's prison in the country are still in the early phase. It is more like a village than a prison with a series of houses set in pleasant grounds surrounded by a high-security fence. Freedom to walk around the complex is granted to all but those who are socially difficult, disruptive or just out to make trouble. A separate block, Bleak House, is set aside to cope with the more difficult element and solitary confinement is also an option. Prisoners are allowed to wear their own clothes, encouraged to pursue activities such as sewing, cooking and gardening and, towards the end of a sentence, they are encouraged to work in the local community.

In 1981 the prison was the focus of a fly-on-the-wall television documentary, *Living In Styal*, and is believed to have been the inspiration behind the long-running fictional series about women's prisons, *Within These Walls*. Although Styal has many excellent qualities, it has had its fair share of incidents of lesbianism, drug taking and inmate suicides.

The prison hit the national headlines when in a period of twelve months (August 2002–August 2003) there were six suicides. In one reported incident five women broke into a prison medicine cabinet and ingested medication. One died in the prison but the other four were saved after being rushed to hospital.

The six suicides represented more than half of the total prison deaths in the UK in one year and prompted not only newspaper headlines but also questions in the House of Commons, an investigation by Cheshire police and an investigation by the Home Office under the control of the Prisons and Probation Ombudsman.

An area of deep concern was the possibility that many of the women who commit suicide in prison should not be there in the first place. Alcoholics, drug dependants and those with mental health problems require a level of skill and care not always available in prisons. The investigations recognised that more work and support was needed in this specialist area. Current conditions in Styal Prison are more in keeping with the modern age. Health problems and drug issues are addressed and there is even dietary advice on offer.

Styal Women's Prison has over its short history had several infamous murderers within its walls: Mary Bell and Myra Hindley to name but two. Sally Clark, who was scandalously convicted and then declared innocent of the murder of her two infant sons, was also briefly remanded there. Following her conviction for the attempted murder of two of the elderly patients under her care in Leighton Hospital, Crewe, Mrs Barbara Salisbury was sentenced to five years' imprisonment in June 2004 and taken to Styal.

BRUCHE POLICE TRAINING COLLEGE

Another centre, which was previously regarded as a bastion for the protection of standards of the British way of life, came under the national microscope in a shatteringly negative way. In October 2003, Bruche Police Training College near Warrington featured in the national news when the sensational findings of an undercover journalist were broadcast, revealing that the college harboured some police recruits who openly confessed to each other that they were racist and hostile to ethnic minorities on the basis of colour. Unsurprisingly, the revelations caused shock waves throughout the land and particularly within the police force.

The centre at Bruche trains recruits from the north-west, Greater Manchester, North Wales and Cheshire for four months. Undercover reporter Mark Daly enlisted as a recruit, completed his training undetected, and then started working as a probationary constable at Hazel Grove, near Stockport. During his training and while working on probation, Daly filmed his experiences with a miniature camera and sound recorder.

What emerged was a shocking indictment of a police force that had taken what they thought to have been stringent measures to eliminate racism and religious discrimination. Television viewers across the nation watched as Daly revealed the conversations he had recorded with his unaware fellow trainees

Bruche Police Training College, near Warrington. *(Bob Burrows)*

for the BBC television programme *The Secret Policeman*. Seven officers from Cheshire, Greater Manchester, and North Wales were named and quoted. The conversations were spattered with racist comments and, as if to underline their bigotry, one filmed sequence showed a trainee policeman wearing a white Ku Klux Klan hood.

Mark Daly was finally exposed while working at Hazel Grove and was himself arrested for obtaining earnings by deception and for damaging police property.

The police reaction to the revelations was at first disappointing, seeming more concerned at the methods used by the BBC to seek out the truth, accusing the organisation, among other things, of wasting public money.

However, later statements confirmed that the police were totally committed to eliminating bigotry and racism from the force and outlined steps and policy already in place, which served to indicate that the first reaction had been one of hurt and embarrassment. Nevertheless, the shock waves from the exposure were all-embracing and all-consuming. The Home Office, MPs locally and nationally, the media and the public were unanimous in their condemnation of the vitriolic and dangerous views expressed at the college. Apologies were made to the Jewish Association of Police Officers and to the British public by the police force.

Follow-up action as a result of the programme was swift and a series of investigations were launched including one into the standard of police training at the college. Almost at once five recruits involved in the investigation resigned from the force and three more were suspended. Unquestionably the fly-on-the-wall programme was a devastating blow to the Police Federation, which had been fighting hard to respond to allegations from some quarters that racism in the police force was institutionalised. However, it must be recorded that although the racist revelations were a shock to those who believed that real progress had been made in the force with regard to the just and fair treatment of ethnic minorities, it was only a view expressed by a tiny minority. The vast majority of the British police force are conscientious and fair-minded in their treatment of the general public and our ethnic minorities and only good will come from the shocking bigotry and bile revealed on *The Secret Policeman*.

The Crown Prosecution Service later ruled that there was insufficient evidence to bring charges of racism against five of the recruits, including two from the Cheshire force, but nine of the offending police trainees involved in the original film have resigned and are now out of the police force. A report produced in 2005 cast doubt upon the future of Bruche as a training centre when it recommended its closure. It would seem that the stigma associated with Bruche and the quality of training required for future police recruits could never now be compatible.

ACCIDENT BLACK SPOT

Cheshire has the dubious claim of being home to the most dangerous road in Britain, as revealed by the European Road Assessment Programme in October 2003. The A537, a Pennine route running from Macclesfield to Buxton with the Cat and Fiddle pub, the highest in Britain, at its summit, is infamous for the number of fatal and near fatal accidents that have occurred on its undulating highway.

The A537 across the Peak District is the most dangerous road in Britain. *(Bob Burrows)*

The winding, undulating A537, a favourite with bikers. *(Bob Burrows)*

The assessment programme showed that from 1999 to 2001 there had been thirty-five serious accidents, the same number as from 1996 to 1999. The statistics for 2001–3 show some improvement with twenty serious accidents, but that is still a terrible indictment for a stretch of road whose beauty belies its reputation as the 'Road to Hell'.

This scenic, winding, undulating, mountainous road makes its way through the spectacular Peak District moors and hills. In the winter it can at times be impassable but in the summer the road is a joy – that is if you're not involved in a serious accident. The bikers who travel great distances to race down the A537 are not there to appreciate the view. They enjoy the thrill of roaring around numerous, narrow bends, then accelerating at great speed on the rare straight stretches, overtaking cars and heavy transport vehicles, before hitting the next hairpin bend. The road has a roller-coaster, switch-back image, but on many occasions the ride has ended in tragedy. Over the past eight years at least five motorbike riders have been killed and thirty more seriously injured, some crippled for life. The A537 has been referred to as the 'poor man's' Isle of Man TT challenge.

Cheshire County Council has tried to improve conditions on the road, investing in new signs, chevrons and crash barriers, and has attempted to straighten out some of the bends. Nevertheless, maintaining the 13 miles of road under its jurisdiction is an expensive project. The police are also playing their part. High-profile patrols, mobile cameras on certain dangerous stretches and a 50mph speed limit has helped to reduce the number of fatalities and led to the improved statistics. Only one death has been recorded since December 2001: a Macclesfield man was killed after his motorbike collided with a red Nissan Micra in September 2004.

The accident occurred close to the Setter Dog public house at Walker Barn when the motorbike travelling towards Buxton was in collision with the car travelling in the opposite direction. The car driver escaped with minor injuries but the bike rider was killed. Despite this latest setback, the police are determined that the vast improvement in the safety record of the A537 will continue and it will cease to be a notorious accident black spot altogether.

LINDOW MAN

There is a much older site in Cheshire which had until recently hidden its infamy well. Lindow Moss, situated down quiet Cheshire country lanes at Knolls Green, between Mobberley and Wilmslow, has had several of its dark secrets uncovered over the past twenty years. But how many more lie undiscovered beneath its dark, soggy, peat-rich depths?

The land has revealed evidence of the presence of humans dating back to prehistoric times. In 1884 remains of a man-made causeway constructed from

Lindow Moss, where the body of a man killed in Roman times was uncovered in a peat bog. *(Bob Burrows)*

timbers and logs and used to traverse the watery, boggy ground was uncovered and a similar structure was revealed during excavations for Manchester Airport's second runway. In addition, the surrounding area has from time to time yielded artefacts, such as flints estimated to be more than 3,000 years old. For hundreds of years Lindow Moss has been used for peat extraction, but modern-day encroachment has reduced the 1,400-acre site by 90 per cent. In ancient times it would have been a dark, mysterious place with much more water than today, making the peat bog a dangerous spot, especially in winter. Even today it can be treacherous and people have had to be rescued from certain areas.

In August 1984 Lindow Moss was suddenly thrust into the news with an extraordinary discovery. Men extracting peat unearthed parts of a body. It was not the first time that such a discovery had been made, but when the experts were called in they quickly realised that they were dealing with an exceptional find, which would create worldwide interest. So well was the corpse preserved that at first it was thought to be a recent murder victim. But the leathery body had a thin cord tied tightly around the neck which had been used as a garrotte. Closer examination revealed that the skull had been fractured with two blows to the head, probably from an axe, and the throat had been cut. It was supposed that the corpse had then been dropped into the lake and over the years had become encased in the all-embracing peat.

The victim was about 25 years old, 5ft 7in tall, well built, healthy with neat, well-trimmed fingernails, and all indications were that he came from a privileged background. Experts deduced that he had been the victim of a Druid ritual sacrifice and several indications, including the presence of mistletoe in the body, supported their conjecture.

However, there was real difficulty in establishing just how long the body had lain in the bog due to the preserving qualities of the peat. First calculations suggested that it was more than 2,500 years old, but later calculations dated it from 55 BC to AD 100. The find was unique in so much as it was Britain's only surviving bog body. Television documentaries and the press dubbed the find 'Lindow Man' and 'Pete Marsh'. Today the body can be viewed in the British Museum.

Extraordinary as it was, the find prompted further revelations. In the previous year, 1983, a female head was found in the same area and was thought to have been 1,500 years old. In 1994 other body parts were discovered and some were believed to be from Roman times, until a Wilmslow man who lived close to Lindow Moss went to the police and confessed that several years previously he had murdered his wife and buried the body in the bog.

Lindow Moss is a unique place and there is concern that the area is being continually eroded by peat extraction and needs conserving. But if it had not been for the peat extractors, we would not have discovered Lindow Man. How many more similar sacrifices were made at the site? The peat may yet reveal more of its secrets.

3

DAYS OF INFAMY

This chapter deals with incidents or events, some not strictly infamous, involving or affecting Cheshire-born citizens or residents, which have occurred largely in the county. However, the first one occurred outside the county, in Surrey, and was to have repercussions which continue today.

CRICKET – ENGLAND V AUSTRALIA AT THE OVAL: 28/29 AUGUST 1882

The whole country, and indeed many parts of the world, thrilled to the magnificent cricket between England and Australia in the summer of 2005. The cricketing rivalries between the two countries has endured for more than 120 years. Over the past eighteen years Australia had held the upper hand and when they came to England in 2005 they were indisputably the best team in the world. However, England, playing exciting cricket, beat Australia by

Albert Neilson Hornby, who captained England in both cricket and rugby in 1882. *(Lancashire County Cricket Club)*

two tests to one in the five test match series, thereby regaining The Ashes for the first time in eighteen years. The revival, the renaissance of English cricket, was greeted by an open-bus ticker-tape parade through London, countless television and radio interviews broadcast around the world, a plethora of cricket books and the birth of a whole new era of heroes, Andrew 'Freddie' Flintoff, Michael Vaughan, Kevin Pietersen and Steve Harmison to name just a few. For the first time in many years, young people, male and female, became interested in cricket as they watched the pace and ferocity of the two teams. So what was all the fuss about? The Ashes trophy, a tiny urn that can be held in the palm of one hand, seems a very insignificant trophy for two nations to battle over for more than 120 years. What is Cheshire's connection with this memorable occasion? Over the years many Cestrians have played cricket for England and have battled with Australia over this precious trophy, but it was a Cheshire man who was responsible for the whole tradition.

Albert Neilson Hornby was born in Blackburn in 1847 but shortly afterwards moved to Nantwich, Cheshire, where he printed his name indelibly on British sport. A small man, a mere 5ft 6in tall, he became a giant, a true sporting Corinthian. In 1882 he became the first and only person to

Albert Neilson Hornby was President of Nantwich Cricket Club for more than twenty years. *(Bob Burrows)*

captain England in two major sporting disciplines: cricket and rugby. He was a good boxer, won a road race for a bet and scored a goal in the FA Cup for Blackburn Rovers. He played county cricket for Lancashire for more than thirty years before becoming President of the club, a post that he held in excess of twenty years. Despite his many duties and high profile Hornby took a very active interest in Nantwich Cricket Club, where he also held the position of President for more than twenty years. He was responsible for bringing Lancashire County Cricket Club to Nantwich for an annual fixture, an event which continued for over forty years.

He became a true Cestrian, accepting many duties in his adopted county: he was a captain in the Cheshire Militia, a Cheshire magistrate, the first county councillor and chairman of the Nantwich Conservative Association. Although he was from a rich family with a privileged background, he was universally popular. He was renowned for his sense of justice and fair play and his ability to make decisions. When touring Australia in 1878 Hornby physically defended Lord Hawke who was attacked by a hooligan and in another match he forcibly restrained a thug who was causing damage off the pitch. He was also known as a very competent cricketer, a forcing opening bat, and in 1881 he actually topped the national scoring averages, beating the game's legendary W.G. Grace.

When Australia came to England in 1882 they were regarded as a good side but no real match for England, who not only had Hornby as captain but also the mighty W.G. Grace and R.G. Barlow, Hornby's prolific opening bat partner at Lancashire. When the historic match began, all went well for England at first and Australia were dismissed for only 63 in their first innings and England replied with 101. However, Grace scored four runs and Hornby only two runs, so both failed.

Australia did a little better in the second innings making 122, which left England only requiring 85 runs to win and with Grace, Barlow and Hornby, it would surely be a formality. At one stage England were fifty-one for two wickets down, with the mighty W.G. Grace thirty-two not out. Then disaster struck: Grace was caught out for thirty-two runs and England started to slide. Barlow had already gone, bowled by Spofforth for nought. It was recorded that the tension was such that one spectator dropped dead and another was reported to have chewed through his umbrella handle. English batsmen came to the wicket with ashen faces as the wickets started to tumble. England's last five wickets fell for seven runs and invincible England lost the test match by seven runs.

Australia was naturally overjoyed and their hero Spofforth was carried shoulder-high to the pavilion. Theirs was certainly a great victory but the reaction to the defeat for England was out of all proportion. The popular newspaper of the time, *The Sporting Times*, printed a now-famous obituary notice, which read:

In Affectionate Remembrance
Of
ENGLISH CRICKET
Which Died At The Oval
On
29th AUGUST 1882
Deeply lamented by a large circle of
Sorrowing friends and acquaintances

....

R.I.P.

....

N.B. The body will be cremated and the ashes taken to Australia.

Gravestone of Albert
Neilson Hornby in
the churchyard at
Acton, Nantwich.
He died in 1925.
(Bob Burrows)

So was born the story of The Ashes, a tradition which is now firmly rooted in the history of cricket. At this stage 'The Ashes' were mythical. Later in 1882 England left for Australia to try to regain 'The Ashes'. Technically they failed because the four-match series ended in two wins each. However, after the second test match in Melbourne a group of Melbourne ladies presented the England captain, the Honourable Ivo Bligh, with a small urn. The urn contained the ashes formed from a burnt bail used in the match. Bligh, later to become Lord Darnley, left the urn to the MCC in his will. This then is the trophy, which is competed for every time England plays Australia. The major bone of contention from Australia's point of view is that the urn, The Ashes, always remains at Lord's Cricket Ground irrespective of the winner.

A.N. Hornby, for all his talents and tremendous reputation, is mostly remembered for being England's captain on the infamous day when England lost a test match and created a tradition, a legend that perpetuates to this day. When he died in Nantwich on 17 December 1925 at the age of 78, it seemed as if the whole of Cheshire and more attended his funeral. He was buried in the small churchyard in Acton in his beloved Nantwich. His distinctive headstone: three cricket stumps crossed by a bat with a ball nestling at the foot of a stump carved into the stone, can be clearly seen, and for many years it has been a place of pilgrimage for cricket lovers.

THE ULTIMATE SACRIFICE: 11 FEBRUARY 1957

For the family of John Axon, 11 February 1957 was a day of infamy. But if it had not been for Axon's unselfish action and sacrifice it may well have been a day of even greater disaster resulting in great loss of life. Born in Stockport on 4 December 1900, John Axon had been a railwayman all his working life: cleaner, fireman and finally a driver with the London and North Western Railway, London Midland and Scottish Railway and British Rail.

On the fateful day Axon was in charge of a locomotive carrying more than 500 tons of freight on the Buxton to Warrington route on the London Midland Region line. He knew the line well and as he approached Chapel-en-le-Frith at a steady 15mph he knew that there was a steep gradient, so he prepared to stop the train before making the descent.

Suddenly, without warning, there was a deafening noise and scalding high-pressure steam jetted into his cab. The first discharge hit his legs and feet and he was very badly burnt. The steam pipe had fractured and destroyed the braking system. Driver Axon was well aware of the desperate situation. He could jump and save his own life, after all he had a wife and children to care for, but he realised that a 500-ton train descending at speed was a lethal weapon. He decided to stay and, with the help of his fireman, closed the regulator and applied the handbrake to slow down the train. When this did not work Axon ordered his fireman to jump and stayed on the train as it gathered speed with the steam and boiling water still pouring into the cab.

Conditions were unbearable but he stayed at his post. He managed to wave a warning to a signalman that the train was out of control. He hoped that he might gain control when and if it reached a more favourable gradient. Sadly it was not to be. The runaway train crashed into the rear of another train going in the same direction and Axon was killed. He was awarded the George Cross which, for civilians, is the ultimate award for bravery and is not given lightly. The *London Gazette* of 7 May 1957 stated that 'Driver Axon displayed devotion to duty, fortitude and outstanding courage in highly dangerous and alarming conditions. He gave his life in an attempt to prevent a collision.' Axon received many posthumous accolades, including the *Daily Herald* Order of Industrial Heroism and the Stockport Council Shield for Bravery. In 1981 an electric locomotive was named after him and there was even a song recorded about his bravery, 'Ballad of John Axon'. The family gave the George Cross medal to the National Railway Museum in 1978.

GREAT TRAIN ROBBERY: 1963

Although this incident took place outside Cheshire, one of the central figures in the whole incident, the train driver, came from Crewe.

In 1963 Britain suffered one of the worst robberies in its history and definitely the biggest train robbery ever perpetrated in these islands. The Great Train Robbery occurred on 8 August 1963 and the gang of twenty or so initially got away with £2.3 million, the equivalent of about £42 million today. The robbery spawned a whole industry of books, television documentaries and a film and some of the robbers have featured again and again in the headlines, particularly Ronnie Biggs, as the police pursued them around the world over several decades.

In addition to the criminals, one of the central figures in the whole incident was 57-year-old Jack Mills, the train driver. Little did he know that, as he left his Crewe home that morning to drive his train, he would enter the history books.

The gang planned to rig the train signals near Chaddington village in Buckinghamshire in the early hours of the morning. The train ground to a halt just after 3 a.m. at the rigged signals and when a fireman went to investigate, the waiting gang restricted him. Mills went to find out what had happened to his colleague. He too encountered the gang. He struggled to escape and during the fighting he collapsed bleeding heavily from a severe blow to the head. The gang then discovered that their plan to move the train a little way to enable them to offload the money-filled mailbags was thwarted when their alleged train expert found that he couldn't operate a mail train.

Mills, now severely traumatised and hurting from his wounds, was forced to move the train. The gang offloaded more than 120 sacks and offered Mills some of their ill-gotten gains. He refused.

When the police reached the scene the robbers of course had fled. They handcuffed Mills to his driver mate Dave Whitby as a precaution and he was taken to hospital. Mills would spend three days in hospital having his four wounds attended to. A bruised arm and a black eye added to his head injuries and he was later transferred to the railways' convalescent home in Dawlish where he spent three weeks recuperating.

The gang all escaped to a barn in Leathersalde, Oxfordshire, to wait for the hue and cry to die down. As the police started to close in, the gang dispersed to all parts of the globe. Despite their apparently successful operation they had carelessly left behind vital clues. Fingerprints on cups and bowls in the barn and one on the train itself. The police were quickly on to them and over the years thirteen of them were captured and sentenced to prison terms ranging from twenty to thirty years each. Many of the public thought that the sentences were a little severe. However, the judge concentrated on the violence used against Mills, dispelling any romantic ideas of a daring, audacious deed. He summarised: 'This is nothing less than a sordid crime of violence, inspired by vast greed; anybody who has seen the nerve-shattered engine driver can have no doubt of the terrifying effect on the law abiding citizen of a concerted assault by masked and armed robbers in darkness.'

Perhaps the most famous of the robbers was Ronnie Biggs who was captured but then escaped from Wandsworth prison and fled to Spain, then to Australia and finally Brazil where he remained until 2001. He returned to the UK hoping to be pardoned but was arrested and imprisoned to complete his original twenty-five-year sentence.

Mills was universally hailed as a hero for trying to resist the robbers and for refusing their offer of a share. Suffering from his injuries he was placed on lighter duties by the Post Office, but was only given £250 as a reward. A public fund was set up which raised £34,000 and enabled Jack and his wife to buy a bungalow in his home town of Crewe. Sadly he died of leukaemia in February 1970 aged 64. The coroner certified that the injuries sustained by him on that fateful morning of 8 August 1963 had not contributed to nor caused his death. Shortly afterwards a journalist, Peta Fordham, who wrote a book about the train robbery, felt free to break a promise she said she had made to Jack Mills several years before. The robbers had always maintained that they had not used serious force against Mills and indeed Mills had told a reporter that apart from the initial struggle and blow to the head they had treated him like a gentleman. It is alleged that Mills had told Peta Fordham that although he had been hit on the back of the head during the fighting which caused severe bleeding, the more serious injury to his head occurred as he fell to the floor, hitting his head on a steel dashboard. He had begged

Fordham not to reveal this information as he feared that the news that the more serious wound was accidental would adversely affect his pension. She had kept the secret knowing that the truth did not alter the fact that the robbers were guilty, but she was well aware that it may have helped to reduce some of the long sentences meted out to the gang.

In his evidence Mills stated, 'a masked man entered the cab holding a stick as though he was going to strike me. I grappled with the man. Then someone who came in through the other cab door struck me from behind. Next thing I remember I was on my knees.' It is still believed that the man who actually struck that blow has never been identified or even caught. No matter the eventual degree of injury, Mills was subjected to a violent attack with a clear intent to disable him. He could have died instantly. Jack Mills remains a victim of Britain's biggest and most notorious train robbery.

DEATH OF A HERO: 12 JUNE 1965

Another train incident occurred on 5 June 1965 and only the unselfish actions of a brave man prevented a very serious accident which would have resulted in the deaths or very serious injury of many rail passengers.

On that fateful day Wallace Arnold Oakes, born in Barbridge near Nantwich on 23 April 1932, was the driver of a steam locomotive that left Crewe pulling ten coaches. Barely minutes into the journey, when the train was travelling at about 60mph, a blow-back from the engine firebox suddenly filled the cab with acrid smoke and fumes. The fireman managed to force his way out through a side window and onto the cab steps where he was able to extinguish his burning clothes. He could not see into the cab but he realised that the brake had been applied as the train was slowing.

The train stopped just short of Winsford and the fireman clambered back into the cab as the flames subsided. He found his colleague, Driver Wallace Oakes, lying on the floor of the cab, his body severely burnt. Later examination revealed that he had more than 80 per cent burns. He was still alive and able to speak. Investigators arriving on the scene found that the brake had been fully applied, the regulator was partly open and the blower valve was fully open. It was apparent that despite the choking smoke and fumes and the searing heat, Driver Oakes had remained at the controls and had ensured that the train was in a safe state before collapsing with appalling injuries. He was well aware of the risk he was taking, but his brave actions had ensured the safety of his passengers.

Tragically, Wallace Oakes, who lived at Wheelock Heath, Sandbach, died from his injuries a week later on 12 June 1965 at Wythenshawe Hospital. His ultimate sacrifice was recognised by the award of the George Cross, which his widow Dorothy received from the Queen on 16 November 1965. In addition he was awarded the Bronze Medal from the Carnegie Hero Trust in 1966. Plaques were erected at his old school, Acton Primary, and at Crewe Station commemorating his brave action and his memory.

On 19 February 1981, in a ceremony conducted by the General Secretary of ASLEF, Ray Buckton, at Euston Station, British Rail officials named an electric locomotive 'Driver Wallace Oakes GC' in a fitting tribute to a brave man. For the Oakes family, 5 June 1965 was a day of infamy but if it had not been for the bravery and dedication of Driver Oakes it may well have been a day of infamy for many more families.

STOCKPORT AIR CRASH: 4 JUNE 1967

The passengers were relaxed and happy, perhaps not too happy, as their British Midlands Airways Argonaut holiday jet started its descent on a grey, wet, June morning towards Manchester Airport, signifying the end of their holiday. Overhead lockers closed, seat belts secured, seats in upright position – all was in order as the holidaymakers faced up to the prospect of returning to work.

But the controlled descent through the low cloud suddenly turned to disaster as a fuel pump malfunctioned, causing a fire to break out in the two left engines. The pilot, Harry Marlow, fought hard to regain control. He could see Stockport spread out below him. Vehicles moving along the highways, the streets busy with people, packed residential areas, schools, office blocks, factories; he knew instantly that he was juggling with a catastrophe. Realising that a crash was inevitable, he managed to steer the stricken falling jet away from a block of flats and a gasometer. Nevertheless it hit the ground like a huge bomb between Hopes Carr and Waterloo Road, just half a mile from Stockport town centre. The devastation was instant. Shattered wreckage, burning fuel, smoke and fumes greeted the first rescuers. The real horror for those first on the scene was the image of passengers trapped in their seats, unable to escape the spreading flames. Helpless, many died while their would-be rescuers could only look on in anguish, powerless to save them. It was a memory which would haunt them for years to come. Of the eighty-four passengers and crew on board the Argonaut that June morning, only twelve survived the carnage.

The Stockport air crash was a disaster in which seventy-two people lost their lives, but it could very well have been a major catastrophe. The plane missed the town centre, flats and a gasometer and largely due to the pilot's efforts landed in an area in which no deaths were caused on the ground. That in itself was a minor miracle. There were a number of stories of personal bravery concerning rescuers who put their lives at risk in desperate attempts to pull passengers from the blazing inferno. Police officer Bill Oliver is believed to have been the first man on the spot and he managed to release several people from the wreckage.

The scene of devastation after a holiday jet crashed between Hopes Carr and Waterloo Road, Stockport, on 4 June 1967. *(Stockport Express)*

Investigators sift through the wreckage of the British Midlands plane after it crashed half a mile from Stockport town centre, 1967. *(Stockport Express)*

Another man, Brian Quinn, got a ladder and was able to get into the fuselage. Eventually the flames and the risk of an explosion forced the rescuers to abort their desperate efforts. The pilot was among the twelve survivors. The site of the crash is now commemorated with a civic memorial and a blue plaque acknowledging the role of the many brave rescuers.

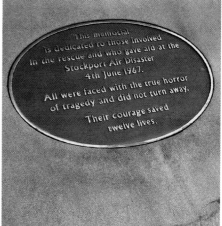

Above left: A memorial plaque in memory of the seventy-two people who died in the Stockport air crash, 1967. *Right:* A plaque dedicated to the rescuers involved in the aftermath of the Stockport air crash in 1967. *(Bob Burrows)*

The site of the 1967 air disaster: Hopes Carr and Waterloo Road, Stockport, today, showing the memorial, centre. *(Bob Burrows)*

TELEVISION INTERVIEW SHOCKER: 1 DECEMBER 1976

Marple's highly respected television presenter Bill Grundy featured in what is still, even in these more permissive days, regarded as one of the most notorious interviews ever broadcast on a live national programme.

Grundy established himself in the north-west area with his punchy, blunt style, which was ideal for soccer commentary and interviews. Soon he attracted national interest and moved south to work for Thames Television.

On 1 December 1976 he conducted a live interview with the four members of the punk rock band the Sex Pistols who were already notorious for their aggressive attitude. Tattooed, with spiky hair, earrings and a complete disregard for normal standards of behaviour, they were crowded together in the small cramped studio with several of their fans including members of the band Siouxsie Sioux.

From the outset Grundy appeared ill at ease and very soon into the interview the 'F' word was introduced into the conversation followed shortly by Sex Pistols band member Johnny Rotten being sarcastic to Grundy and uttering an expletive under his breath. Grundy asked him to repeat it and he did, 'shit'. The interview staggered on and in what appeared to be a moment of desperation Grundy turned to the girl fans standing behind the group and asked if they were enjoying themselves.

Bill Grundy, television presenter, whose interview with the Sex Pistols in 1976 shocked the nation. *(Stockport Express)*

Sioux said to him, 'I always wanted to meet you.'

Grundy replied, 'Did you really? We'll meet afterwards, shall we?'

Steve Jones, one of the Sex Pistols, abused Grundy, saying 'You dirty sod. You dirty old man!'

Grundy, 'Well, keep going, chief, keep going. Go on, you've another five seconds. Say something outrageous.'

Jones, 'You dirty bastard.'

Grundy, 'Go on, again.'

Jones, 'You dirty fucker.'

Grundy (by now really rattled and beyond recovery), 'What a clever boy!'

Jones, 'What a fucking rotter.'

Grundy (now trying desperately to close the show), 'Well, that's it for tonight. The other rocker, Eamonn, and I'm saying nothing else about him, will be back tomorrow. I'll be seeing you soon.'

Turning to the band, 'I hope I'm not seeing you again. From me though, goodnight.' As the signature tune faded Grundy muttered curses knowing that the interview had been a disaster.

The following day the interview featured in all the tabloids and there was one memorable front-page headline in the *Daily Mirror* which screamed out, 'The Filth And The Fury'. Grundy was hauled over the coals for allowing the programme to get out of hand and for what appeared to be his goading of the group to say outrageous things. It would appear that his goading was nothing more than a loss of nerve and frankly not knowing how to cope with people who were prepared to ignore convention. For him the incident was just a blemish on a distinguished career, but unfortunately it does appear in the annals of television history and regrettably it is what he is most remembered for. Grundy died in 1993.

The Sex Pistols did not escape scot-free. A number of promoters and agents were put off by their unpredictability and they were banned from a number of venues. Johnny Rotten resurfaced in 2004 with his appearance on the television programme *I'm A Celebrity Get Me Out Of Here*.

POLICE KILL SERIAL KILLER: RAINOW 1977

On a particularly severe snowy winter's night many of the villagers in the tiny hilly hamlet of Rainow just outside Macclesfield answered their doors to find a policeman standing, shivering, on their doorstep.

Bill and Patsy Faulkner were residents of Rainow on that evening, Friday 14 January 1977, and recall the policeman asking, 'Do you own any firearms?' and the more chilling warning as he left, 'Lock your doors and do not venture out tonight.' The hamlet's residents were aware that something serious was happening but did not know the extent of events. The police had,

On the night of 14 January 1977 heavy snow made this request to drive slowly through Rainow irrelevant. *(Bob Burrows)*

in fact, placed a cordon around the village and set up roadblocks which were manned by armed officers. Unbeknown to the residents a highly dangerous, armed, serial killer was heading towards Rainow along the A6 from Derbyshire with a terrified female hostage whose entire family he, unknown to her, had butchered.

William Thomas Hughes had escaped from police custody after stabbing one of the officers in the neck with a knife. He then forced the driver of the taxi, which had been taking him and his police escort from Leicester Prison to Chesterfield Magistrates Court, to drive to the village of Stone Edge. He forced the three men out of the car and was then free to complete his escape. Tragically for Richard and Gill Moran and their family, Hughes happened upon their lonely farmhouse, Pottery Cottage, at Eastman near Chesterfield. It was later revealed that for three days he held the Morans and their 10-year-old daughter and Mrs Moran's parents as terrified hostages in their own home. He tied the family to chairs in different rooms and then forced himself upon Gill Moran, threatening to kill her family if she did not look after him. She was made to cook and cater to his needs. Eventually she managed to alert a neighbour who called the police. They responded quickly and surrounded the house.

Hughes was asked to give himself up but he refused. After he threatened to kill Gill Moran with an axe, the police let him drive away with her in a bronze Chrysler saloon. They pursued him at high speed until Hughes's car skidded off the snowy road at Tideswell Moor. Surrounded by police, he once again threatened to kill his hostage and held a knife against her throat. Once again the police had little option but to accede to his demands and this time they gave him one of their unmarked cars.

The pursuit continued through Chapel-en-le-Frith, Whaley Bridge, and Furness Vale. Meanwhile, back at Pottery Cottage the police entered the house and discovered a horrific scene. Gill Moran's husband, her daughter and her father had been cold-bloodedly stabbed to death in the chairs in which they had been bound. The police found the body of Gill's mother, also stabbed to death, in the garden where she had presumably tried to escape. Despite his promises to Gill Moran, Hughes had callously and brutally butchered her defenceless family.

The villagers in the snowbound hills of Rainow, warm and snug in their houses, were aware that something was afoot, but were unaware that a serial killer was heading their way. The police had by now set up a road block at the entrance to the village near the Rainow Institute by placing a single-decker bus across the road against a 6ft snow drift, covering any gaps with police cars. Several police marksmen were strategically positioned while others who had borrowed shotguns from the villagers placed themselves behind barricades. The trap was set.

Hughes, pursued by police cars, descended the hill and could see spread out below him the lights of the houses, twinkling like an oasis in the wintry night. He also spotted the barricades and, far from stopping, he accelerated, scraped and skidded alongside the bus, mounted the icy kerb, propelling a smashed road sign in front of him, before grinding to a halt after hitting a stone wall.

For a time there was silence. As the officers approached the car Hughes smashed a window and threw himself across Gill Moran, warning the police

The road along which serial killer William Thomas Hughes approached the hamlet of Rainow. *(Bob Burrows)*

The site of the police ambush in Rainow during which Hughes was shot. *(Bob Burrows)*

Pottery Cottage, Eastman, near Chesterfield, where Hughes held the Morans hostage before killing four members of the family. *(Derbyshire Evening Telegraph)*

Gill Moran and her husband Richard, who was killed by Hughes at their lonely cottage in 1977. *(Manchester Evening News)*

that he would kill her. The terrified woman begged the police to 'keep away'. For a time there was a stand-off as the police kept their distance before striking up a dialogue with the killer. Patiently he was asked to release his prisoner on a promise that the police would help him as much as possible. Hughes asked for cigarettes, shoes and another vehicle. His requests were met but the police insisted that this time, although they would give him another car, he would not be allowed to take his hostage with him.

Villagers who witnessed the scene remembered that there was silence for about thirty seconds and then a single shot, frantic screams and a volley of more shots shattered the quiet. Hughes had insisted that the police surrounding his car show themselves before he came out to change cars. Unbeknown to him there were three more policemen stationed behind him. Inspector Howse of the Derbyshire police rushed the car, as he believed that he saw Hughes attempting to kill Gill Moran. While he grappled with Hughes who was attacking him and Moran with an axe, other officers rushed the car and several shots were fired into Hughes at point-blank range. Gill Moran, who had wounds to her forehead and hands, was rushed to Macclesfield Infirmary, shocked and dazed. She was later given the terrible news that Hughes had killed her family. Following a police inquiry the officers involved in the action were exonerated and the slaying of Hughes was declared justifiable homicide.

Chief Superintendent Arthur E. Morris of Cheshire police commended the action of all of the policemen from Cheshire and Derbyshire and praised their efficiency on such a terrible winter's night in such dreadful emotional circumstances. A Home Office investigation was authorised to determine just how such a notorious violent criminal such as Hughes was able to arm himself with a knife and escape from two prison officers. The hamlet of Rainow will never forget the fateful day a serial killer came calling.

SUICIDE OF IAN CURTIS, POP STAR: 18 MAY 1980

The world of music was shocked by the suicide on Sunday 18 May 1980, of Macclesfield pop star Ian Curtis, seemingly at the height of his career. Curtis, born in Macclesfield in 1957 and educated at King's School, had formed, along with another Macclesfield man Stephen Morris, the hugely successful pop group Joy Division.

The group had a massive hit in the 1970s, 'Love Will Tear Us Apart', followed by another big seller 'Unknown Pleasures' in 1979. Joy Division had enjoyed a spell of sell-out tours and Ian was resting at his Macclesfield home in Barton Street. His estranged wife Deborah called at the house that fateful morning with their daughter, found his body and ran out into the street screaming. Curtis, only 23, had hanged himself, presumably in a fit of depression. He left a note, 'At this very moment, I wish I were dead. I just can't cope any more.' Sad that the maker of such beautiful music should have been driven to such a tragic end.

After his death the group re-formed and enjoyed great success as New Order. Fans have remained loyal to Curtis whose memorial stone, inscribed 'Ian Curtis, 18–5–80, Love Will Tear Us Apart' is placed in Macclesfield Cemetery and is frequently visited by people from all over the world, including America and Japan in particular.

Pop star Ian Curtis's memorial stone in Macclesfield Cemetery. *(Bob Burrows)*

MANCHESTER AIR DISASTER: 1985

Manchester Airport was opened by Manchester Corporation in 1928 on what was the first municipal aerodrome in the UK at a small site at Ringway, Cheshire. This temporary structure became permanent in 1935 and scheduled flights were instigated in 1938. Further development followed and flights to New York started in 1953. Since those early days expansion has been dramatic and Manchester has become the second largest airport in the UK. A new runway was established in 1967 to accommodate larger jets. In a major project the Wilmslow–Altrincham road was diverted under a tunnel, allowing the new jets to scream in and land overhead. In 1975 the enlarged airport was officially named Manchester International Airport and throughout the 1980s it was the fastest-growing airport in Europe. The 1990s saw the introduction of a second terminal which cut into large swathes of the lush green Cheshire countryside. Objections were passionate and determined, but were finally overcome. The balance had to be struck between new jobs, prosperity and opportunity for many, against noise and traffic pollution eating into well-established, desirable residential areas. Manchester International Airport is entirely within the historic boundaries of Cheshire and has, over the years, been relatively clear of major disasters.

Firemen battle to extinguish the blaze aboard a holiday jet at Manchester International Airport, 1985. *(Manchester Evening News)*

That was until 22 August 1985 when the airport experienced its greatest disaster. On that fateful morning, a British Airtours Boeing 737 with 137 passengers on board sat patiently on the runway waiting to take off. The passengers were understandably excited as they sat, strapped into their seats, looking forward to flying to the Greek island of Corfu.

The pilot revved up the engines in preparation for take-off and very quickly became aware of a problem. Believing that a tyre had burst, he was prepared to abort the take-off. In fact an engine had failed and a torn fuel line had started a fire which was fanned into action as the plane moved along the runway. Flames and smoke poured from the fuselage as rescuers rushed to the scene. Aboard the aircraft excitement had turned to fear as the deadly smoke and fumes entered the cabin. Blinded by the smoke and choking from the fumes, the passengers desperately fought to reach safety.

Tragically, fifty-five people lost their lives that morning sitting in the stricken aircraft on the tarmac. It was perhaps a miracle that eighty-two people survived the inferno.

FIFTH TEST MATCH, THE OVAL ENGAND v WEST INDIES: 9 AUGUST 1991

The incident that occurred at the Oval in 1991 would more likely be regarded as entertaining rather than infamous, but it deserves a mention.

Brian Johnston, the late great doyen of British cricket broadcasters, was commentating on Friday 9 August at the England v West Indies test match together with colleague Jonathan Agnew. At about 6.30 p.m. the match was abandoned for the day due to bad light and the programme producer instructed Johnston to go through the day's scorecard with Agnew supplying comment and support. What followed has gone down in the annals as one of the greatest ten minutes of spontaneous broadcasting in history. It has been played back and spoken about on many occasions and the BBC to its great credit did not try to go off the air but let it run to the great enjoyment of the vast majority of listeners.

Johnston started to go through the day's scorecard as instructed, describing who had got out and how and how many runs they had made. Agnew dutifully added his comments and all was going according to plan until Johnston came to explain Ian Botham's unfortunate dismissal, hit wicket. Johnston said Botham was out just as he was getting set for a big score and commented how extraordinary his dismissal was. Agnew said, 'Yes, he was just loosening up but I was surprised that he tried to hook the bouncer from Ambrose. In fact I think it hit his helmet.' In attempting the hook Botham had lost his balance and Agnew said that he tried to step over his wicket and he knew what was going to happen. Johnston chipped in saying Botham had tried to do the splits to avoid stepping on his wicket but his inner thigh must have brushed the wicket and removed a bail. It was at that point that Agnew came out with the moment-defining comment, 'He just didn't quite get his leg over.'

For a few seconds Johnston carried on with his summary but in the background there were audible sounds of stifled giggling. Very soon Johnston was infected and he stumbled and sniggered through the next few moments trying valiantly to stop from laughing out loud. At one point he begged, 'Aggers, do stop', and tried to carry on with his voice shaking while barely controlled giggling came from Agnew. Again Johnston begged, 'Aggers for goodness sake, stop it', before giving in and dissolving into laughter. Agnew bravely tried to intervene by continuing with the scorecard in an artificially high squeaky voice, which did not remotely disguise the pressure he was under. He gave in and the pair of them dissolved into fits of giggles until finally Johnston was able to blurt out, 'England all out 419'.

Schoolboy humour, yes, a little childish, well, yes, but at the same time hugely enjoyable. It was comforting to know that a broadcaster with the experience and expertise of Johnston was still capable of succumbing to such puerile humour. Brian Johnston died in 1994 – a great loss to broadcasting. But what of the Cheshire connection?

Jonathan Agnew was born in Macclesfield, Cheshire, in 1960 and as a fast bowler he played for Leicestershire from 1978 to 1990 and also represented England against the West Indies, Australia and Sri Lanka in 1984–5. The experience of broadcasting alongside Brian Johnston despite the 1991 'misdemeanour' obviously stood him in good stead, as he later became the BBC cricket correspondent for Radio 4 and head of *Test Match Special*. His job takes him all around the world commenting on the game he loves. He has never forgotten that August day in 1991 and neither have the vast majority of cricket fans who prefer our national game to be played with a smile.

IRA ATTACK ON WARRINGTON: MARCH 1993

It's hard enough coping with accidents and disasters beyond our control but it is even harder trying to understand the rationale behind deliberate atrocities perpetrated against an innocent, civilian population, no matter what the idealogical struggle allegedly behind such an action.

Readers will no doubt be familiar with the aims and ideals of the Irish Republican Army (IRA). In 1993 the IRA targeted Warrington with an atrocity to enforce its message and obtain headlines for its cause.

A serious incident on the night of 26 February 1993 may have contributed to a feeling that the IRA had made its statement in Warrington and the danger had passed. A policeman pulled over a motorist and as he approached the white van he was shot three times in cold blood. The officer was rushed to hospital and the hunt for the men resulted in two of the gang being apprehended while a third got away. Success was tinged with the realisation of what the gang had really been up to when at about 4 a.m. three large explosions ripped through the early morning air blowing up the Winwick Road gasworks and lighting up the surrounding area. It was later discovered that another device, which could have caused far more serious damage, had failed to detonate. If the public and the security forces thought that they had now had their share of trauma and the IRA would move on to a newer location their hopes were to be cruelly dashed.

Just over three weeks later, on 20 March, a bright, sunny morning was lifting everyone's spirits as they went about their business. The main shopping area, Bridge Street, was particularly full and it was noticeable that there were many families about as the weekend included Mother's Day. Unbeknown to the citizens of Warrington, two of the men who were in Bridge Street that morning were not interested in spring, Mother's Day or the welfare of children or anything else. Their thoughts were set on murder and destruction

Front page of the *Warrington Guardian* after the IRA attack, 1993. *(Warrington Guardian)*

as they placed explosive devices in two litterbins in the middle of the busy shopping centre. They were well aware of the carnage that would follow.

The first device was triggered and naturally sent people into a panic and, as they rushed for safety, many of them ran into the second device, which exploded with great force. Despite the carnage there were only two deaths, tragically children. The atrocity received worldwide coverage by press and other media, but it was the local press, the *Warrington Guardian*, which achieved national recognition for its coverage and indeed won several awards including Team of the Year at the British Press Awards in 1994. The current editor (2006), Nicola Priest, was part of the team that day and remembers the occasion vividly:

> Reporters and photographers were quickly on the scene and as everyone was trying to leave the town, the *Guardian* journalists were trying to get into the town to investigate and report on the bombings. Staff even scaled the 6ft high railings to our building – on the same street as the bombs – to get in as a police cordon was set up around it.

Photographer Mike Boden was named British Press Photographer of the Year for his work and one of his photographs, a particularly harrowing picture of the aftermath, with people yelling and rushing away from the scene as others examined the injured, circulated around the world.

It was the first time that a weekly regional newspaper had received such high recognition from its peers and to receive three 'Oscars' was particularly outstanding. The third award was Journalist of the Year, which went to Mark Rossiter. It was acknowledged that for a local newspaper to cover a disaster on its own territory was more difficult than for a national outside reporter who can be dispassionate and care only for the story without cognisance of the local people and their environs. The local paper had been sensitive and had handled the story with great professionalism.

Following the huge public outcry from all quarters, it is believed that the IRA changed their tactics on the mainland, and stopped targeting the public. The leader of the IRA unit responsible for the attack was captured and sentenced to thirty-five years in prison.

The parents of the murdered children were instrumental in raising funds for a lasting memorial to their sons and in March 2000, the Peace Centre in Warrington was opened to educate young people to understand and tolerate diversity.

Warrington itself has healed its wounds, rebuilt the shopping centre and in doing so received several awards from planners. Bridge Street is once again a throbbing, bustling shopping centre with a memorial in its centre and a plaque to the memory of the two youngsters who were murdered on that infamous spring day in 1993.

GUARDIAN SPECIAL EDITION, Monday, March 29th, 1993

WAR ON CHILDREN

UNITED IN LOVE AND SYMPATHY, FAMILIES SAY A SORROWF

A day of sorrow that town will never forge

By Alastair McIntyre

IT WAS a beautiful spring sun on Friday morning...

Warrington

Family broken by IRA give up the child of their dreams

Johnathan's tiny white coffin is carried to the church

As Wilf and Marie Ball, right, head towards the church the strain is obvious

as a mother realises her loss

the heartache becomes too much to bear

FATHER WATCHES HIS SON SLIP QUIETLY AWAY

By Helen Griffiths

A FATHER has told of his family's "absolute agony" before schoolboy Tim Parry's life support machine was switched off.

The Parry family had clung for five days to the hope that 12-year-old Tim would pull through – despite the terrible head injuries he received in the Warrington bombings outrage.

But as each day went by, that flicker of hope receded.

Doctors told the Great Sankey family on Thursday morning that Tim was clinically dead and asked the family to consider switching off the life-support machine.

"It was absolute agony," said personnel director Colin Parry, aged 37.

"We thought at first that Tim seemed capable of beating this We became very optimistic – then came the realisation that all hope had gone.

Miracle

"You desperately hope that a miracle might happen."

Colin and his wife, Wendy, and their two other children, Dominic, aged 14, and Abigail, 11, spent two hours at Liverpool's Walton Hospital saying their goodbyes.

They squeezed Tim's hands, then left the room in tears. Only his father remained in the hospital unit when the life support system was switched off.

A courageous Mr. Parry said: "He just lay there and quietly slipped away. It was most unlike Tim, because he was normally such a noisy, impudent chap. It wouldn't have surprised me if he had sat up and shouted Vironimo as he went.

"But he went ever so quietly and it was very peaceful. I have to say I was extremely moved."

The Parrys thanked hospital staff at Walton and Warrington and paid a special tribute to Dubliner Susan McHugh, the woman who led a 1,000-strong rally against IRA atrocities last week.

"It's going to take a lot more people like that to stand up and be counted to make sure other parents don't go through the absolute horror Wendy and I have gone through," Mr. Parry added.

Colin and Wendy Parry and inset, son Timothy

Police set up secret base for video pro

By Terry Johnson

POLICE have set up a suite at a secret location to examine 37 video tapes which could identify the Warrington bombers.

The tapes have been recovered by investigating officers from shops and car parks in the town centre and show people movement in the morning of the explosions.

Specialist equipment has been brought in to study the 150 hours of tapes in the hope of catching a glimpse of the bombers.

Det. Chief Inspector Mick Holland, head of Warrington CID, said: "A lot of painstaking work needs to be carried out. These video recordings – part of the security operations of shops and car parks – could prove to be valuable.

"Apart from those, there are now 800 separate lines of inquiry. Some of these will be for elimination purposes but others could throw up vital clues as to the persons who committed this outrage."

Police are not saying whether they are looking for men or women bombers...

PICTURES: Eddie Fuller, Mike Boden, Dave Gillespie, and Darren Tudor

Shattered lives: reports in the *Warrington Guardian* on the families caught up in the IRA blast. *(Warrington Guardian)*

GUARDIAN SPECIAL EDITION, Monday, March 29th, 1993   3

FAREWELL TO THE CHILDREN KILLED IN THE IRA BOMBINGS

WAR ON CHILDREN

Hero PC troubled by boys' deaths

HERO policeman Mark Toker ... gunned down by IRA terrorists in Warrington town centre last month — has told how his own injuries paled into insignificance compared with the deaths of Johnathan Ball and Tim Parry.

Speaking of Johnathan's funeral in Grappenhall on Friday, the saddened constable said: "This business has affected me more than the first one. I was shot which was bad enough to do one way but it pales into insignificance compared with a three-year-old getting killed and a second boy dying.

"This has knocked me back more than getting shot myself," he added.

Mark Toker

Grief from senator

IRISH senator Gordon Wilson, whose 20-year-old daughter Marie died in the IRA bombing of a Remembrance Day ceremony at Enniskillen in 1987, expressed his grief at the tragedy as he attended Johnathan Ball's funeral.

The 80-year-old met Johnathan's family last Thursday and prayed them for the service at St. Wilfrid's.

"As soon as I heard about the bomb at Warrington I felt moved to come. We have a lot of killings in Northern Ireland. This one touched me and my wife very much. I wanted to come just to say sorry and offer comfort, sympathy and love," he said.

"I met Johnathan's family last night. They were very welcoming."

Gordon Wilson

Distressed shoppers at the shrine of Johnathan are comforted by the Salvation Army

weeps

Horror and dismay at pointless death

By Alastair McIntyre

THOUSANDS of people came out in force on Friday to pay their last respects to murdered toddler Johnathan Ball — a three year old boy who had everything to live for.

People were left crying as the cortege passed, with feelings of disgust and horror being expressed.

Penny and Les Rustage, who are friends of the Ball family, echoed "We are absolutely gutted. It is such a pointless death.

"Hopefully, some good can eventually come out of this as I would just like to think that such a lovely boy like Johnathan had died for nothing."

When the procession arrived at Bridge Foot, Mr Stan Noseley, stood in dismay and disbelief with his two granddaughters, Jennifer and Lyndsey.

He said: "The whole range of events are very tragic.

"It makes you think when will the troubles all end, as with even such an awful act here in Warrington, the IRA I think will not give up their campaign.

"I want all the troubles and horrors to end for everybody's sake as well as my grandchildrens."

He added: "There is not much more you can say. Nothing has ever happened in the town like this before.

"People should never forget what happened and I feel the council should put some sort of memorial to commemorate where the two youngsters lost their lives."

At St. Wilfrid's Church, near by resident Mrs Meryl Matthews, was out with her two children. She said: "I think everybody is disgusted about what has gone on.

"Now people are fearful. I am also fearful for my children as such an awful act has happened in Warrington.

"My eldest child is only very young, but he knows something has gone on.

"He has started asking questions, but where do you start to explain?

"I do not think any of us understand why Warrington has been attacked, but when children are asking questions, it is very worrying."

However, the thoughts of the day were summed up by Mrs Marjorie Raine from Grappenhall.

Mrs Raine said: "The extend of the damage which has been done will always be with town.

"But our thoughts and sympathy at the moment go out to the families who have lost loved ones in the tragedy."

'I'll always love you'

"I'LL miss you always until we hug again, your best friend, Simon."

That was the final message from three-year-old Simon Barker, the best friend Johnathan Ball leaves behind.

It was with a Thomas the Tank Engine floral arrangement which was placed at Johnathan's graveside.

The youngsters always played together and hugged and kissed each other every time they met.

Will Ball, Johnathan's father, said: "He's got a beautiful friend named Simon and every time he came round they threw their arms around each other and kissed each other."

Simon, aged three, had also left a small white teddy bear with "I Love You" on a red, heart-shaped cushion, at the scene of the bombing.

Murdered soldier's parents share suffering

By Margaret Westhead

THE terrible events of the past week have intensified the grief of a Warrington family bereaved by another IRA atrocity two years ago.

Stephen Beacham, then a 20-year-old soldier with the First King's Regiment, was blown up by terrorists while on duty at a command post in Londonderry in October 1990.

His body lies close to the latest Warrington terrorist victim Johnathan Ball in Fox Covert cemetery.

For Stephen's grieving parents Bill and Pat and stepmother Jeanne, the Bridge Street bomb attack has resurrected their initial emotions of shock, anger and devastating loss.

Break down

Mrs Pat Beacham of Cabul Close, Orford said: "We are distraught for the families of the two boys. No-one knows what they are going through as much as we do.

"Life has never been the same since Stephen was killed. I am sad all the time but I try to put a brave face on it. I will never get over it. I just have to live with it.

"Sometimes I just break down at work. I have my bad days but everyone is marvellous at work. They understand. If it wasn't for my other son Paul I would crack up.

"I am absolutely disgusted at what has happened in Warrington. The people who did this can't be called human beings. I really feel for these families."

The Beachams are writing to the two sets of bereaved parents, offering to meet and help them when they feel ready.

Mr Bill Beacham said the atrocities had resurrected a nightmare for him. On the day of Johnathan Ball's funeral he had cried all day.

Mr Beacham said: "I always expected to die before Stephen. No-one can imagine how terrible it is until it happens to you. Stephen loved his job. He had a premonition that he would die, he told me so on his last leave.

"Before he went back to North-ern Ireland he made a point of seeing everyone, all his relatives and friends. I sensed he wouldn't return, it was the way he looked at me through the car window when I dropped him off at the airport."

The Beachams said they had been given immense support and comfort from the people of Warrington during those first terrible weeks and particularly on the day of Stephen's funeral. They were sure that the same kindness and generosity would sustain the boys' families.

Mrs Jeanne Beacham, Stephen's stepmother said: "The people of Warrington were wonderful to us. The whole town came to a stop on the day of the funeral. We received more than 300 cards. Warrington is a very close and caring community when something like this happens."

Campaign medal for Tim

TIM Parry's brave fight for life, which tragically ended last Thursday, touched the hearts of the world — and a former soldier has showed his feelings by donating his Campaign Service Medal.

By Jane Woodhead

David Squires, aged 27, of Warrington, has asked the Guardian to pass on his medal, which was awarded to him after service in Ireland, to Tim's family.

Mr Squires said: "Words cannot express my feelings. This is the least I can do.

"A medal has been presented to toddler Johnathan

Ball and I do not want Tim to be left out, after his long and hard battle for life."

Mr Squires, who served with the Cheshire Regiment for seven years, spent a year in Ireland, from 1989.

Teenage girls can't hide their emotions at the shrine to Johnathan and Tim

THE DAY A BUSY STREET FELL INTO SILENCE

It was as though the heart of the town had suddenly stopped beating.

The bustle and vibrancy of normal Saturday street activity just arrested.

The time was 12.20pm, and the top end of Bridge Street was a solid mass of silent witnesses.

Young men, old men, babies in push-chairs, teenage girls holding a single red rose, and pensive mums stood round the shrine of flowers outside Boots chemists where two child innocents were mortally wounded by a terrorist bomb, exactly a week earlier.

No baby's cry was heard. Not even a hushed whisper from any of the hundreds of families gathered. No footstep on the paving flags.

The crowd appeared frozen in silence, remembering little Johnathan and Tim, so cruelly struck down.

It was a vigil of great dignity and compassion. One could feel the intensity of the force. A collective power for healing and for peace — rather than a wish for retribution.

A town that has been so terribly stunned and wounded by the visitation of unimagined evil was starting to re-build.

Its confidence and community spirit were returning.

The people of Warrington in mourning, 1993. *(Warrington Guardian)*

A memorial to the victims of the bomb blast in Warrington's Bridge Street. *(Bob Burrows)*

Bridge Street, Warrington, 2005. *(Bob Burrows)*

HIGH NOON AT KNUTSFORD HEATH: 8 APRIL 1997

The two protagonists flanked by their supporters strode purposefully towards each other and as the distance narrowed they slowed before coming to a halt face to face. The first shot was fired by the faithful sidekick of the ambushing gang's leader. Gunfight at the OK Coral? No, this was the scene on 8 April 1997 when Neil Hamilton, the sitting Conservative MP for Tatton for the last fourteen years, came face to face with his challenger and opponent in the forthcoming general election, Martin Bell.

Martin Bell OBE, an international correspondent with the BBC, was standing as an Independent candidate on an anti-sleaze and corruption policy. He was deliberately opposing Neil Hamilton following the allegations levelled at Hamilton by Mohamed Al Fayed that he was guilty of corruption in taking cash for questions in exchange for raising matters in the House of Commons on behalf of Al Fayed himself (see page 113). Hamilton had strenuously denied the charges and while Parliament was awaiting the results of the Downey inquiry, Hamilton had still been selected by the Conservative constituency party to defend Tatton at the general election. Bell had stated that if Hamilton refused to resign then he would oppose him at the election. Bell was now in the Knutsford area campaigning in what was inevitably a high-profile situation much fêted by the media.

On 8 April 1997, the white-suited Bell, surrounded by national journalists and cameramen, was giving a press conference on Knutsford Heath. Walking towards this group was Neil Hamilton with a group of loyal supporters headed by his wife Christine. The first shot was fired by Christine Hamilton who pointedly demanded of Bell, 'Do you believe that a man is innocent until proven guilty?' Bell replied, 'Of course I do but that's not . . .' His voice trailed away as Christine cut him short, having received the answer she was looking for. 'So you accept that my husband is innocent,' she posed.

Bell started, 'I think that there's a lot . . .'; again she cut him off, repeating, 'Do you accept that my husband is innocent?' Bell, looking battered, averted his eyes, 'Look, I'm not going to be ambushed here, let's just see what comes out.'

During this initial sparring Neil Hamilton had not said a word but had continued to stare at his opponent. Bell started to crumble and muttered, 'I don't know, I don't know, I'm standing here . . .'

'Because you are not prepared to wait for the Downey report,' Christine Hamilton interjected. Bell replied, 'Because a lot of people have asked me to stand here. The impetus comes from local people. Let them choose between us.' Christine, a note of obvious disbelief in her voice, said icily, 'I thought it came from a dinner party in London.'

A fresh voice entered the fray, as at last Neil Hamilton interjected, 'I would just like to say then that you are prepared to give me the benefit of the doubt

Longview Hotel, Knutsford, Martin Bell's headquarters for his 1997 election campaign. *(Bob Burrows)*

BBC correspondent Martin Bell stands as an independent candidate in the 1997 election. *(Knutsford Guardian)*

on the allegations made against me?' Bell replied, 'Yes, absolutely, absolutely,' nodding vigorously. Neil Hamilton turned away triumphantly murmuring, 'Good, good,' knowing that their ambush had succeeded in derailing Martin Bell's campaign, if only for the moment.

The waiting media entourage were unanimous that the Hamiltons had won the showdown on Knutsford Heath. A number of them described the ambush as brilliant. Even Bell responded to Neil Hamilton's apology for hijacking his press conference by saying, 'Well, you haven't done badly.'

The incident appeared damaging to Bell. The media comments on his first press conference were unflattering; indeed one wag described him as 'the prat in the white suit'. It seemed that Hamilton's 32,000-seat majority in the Tatton Conservative stronghold would guarantee him another term as MP.

Press scrum on Knutsford Heath when Martin Bell stood against Neil Hamilton in the 1997 election. *(Knutsford Guardian)*

Although Bell had said that he was not accusing Hamilton of anything, as the campaign proceeded he consistently accused Hamilton of wrongdoing, and despite winning the showdown on Knutsford Heath, Hamilton lost the election to Bell by 11,000 votes – a clear indication that whatever the rights and wrongs of his situation, the public of Tatton had turned against him. And, despite Hamilton's protestations of innocence, the report by Sir Gordon Downey found him guilty as accused.

Face to face: Martin Bell and Neil and Christine Hamilton, Knutsford Heath, 1997. (*Knutsford Guardian*)

TERRORIST TRAGEDY: 14 JANUARY 2003

In January 2003 the small village of Poynton was thrust into the national headlines, tragically underlining the dangers faced by the police in carrying out their duties. Once again terrorists with no respect for human life brought grief to part of Cheshire and devastated a loving family.

Poynton's Special Branch Detective Constable Stephen Oake was killed on 14 January 2003 when he was involved in a police raid on a flat in Crumpsall, Greater Manchester. MI5 had for some time been investigating an Algerian terrorist network which it believed had links to a cell based in London where police had discovered traces of the deadly poison ricin. When the police raided the flat they questioned three men, one of whom had been posing as a student seeking asylum but was believed by the police to be a terrorist. As the officers tried to detain him, one of the men produced a knife and stabbed four of the policemen. Detective Oake's wound proved to be fatal and he died. It was reported afterwards that Stephen Oake had, despite his wound, prevented an even greater tragedy by his bravery and selfless action.

Hundreds of people filled the small Baptist church in Poynton as friends, family and the community turned out to pay tribute to Stephen Oake and to give their support to his widow Lesley and their three children.

GRANDMA BECOMES PRIME SUSPECT: MARCH 2004

An incident that would normally be regarded as laughable were it not so serious occurred in Macclesfield on 5 March 2004.

At about 1.30 a.m. the telephone rang in a small bungalow on the Moss Side estate. The voice warned the occupant, 'We believe that you have a gun and we require you to put up your hands and leave the building.' The occupant was told to look out of the window and accept the advice that the house was surrounded. No resistance was offered and six heavily armed, uniformed, police officers wearing protective body armour entered the small property.

You might think that the police had responded positively to intercept or prevent some atrocity or criminal act. Certainly the response was high powered: the police had alerted the police Armed Response Unit (ARU) which had sent out a SWAT unit and the phone call had been made by a policewoman from the ARU at Winsford. A very smooth, efficient operation, except that the armed and dangerous 'suspect' was a 5ft tall disabled grandmother. She had been hounded by bullies and yobs in her little bungalow for the previous two years. Despite her numerous calls to the police, nothing had been done to stop the harassment, which included breaking her car windows, soiling her garden, and flaunting drugs and alcohol on her front steps.

Yet it would appear that a mischievous phone call (it is presumed from one of the yobs) brought an instant response from a high-powered SWAT unit. All the police found was a digital camera used by the woman to film the hooligans creating a disturbance.

After the incident was featured in many national newspapers, the grandmother finally got a response from officialdom. Action was taken against the yobs and an offer made to move her out of the area. Let us hope that Friday 5 March 2004, infamous as it undoubtedly was, will have positive memories for this woman.

4

INFAMOUS CHARACTERS: MEN

Over the years Cheshire has been the birthplace or the home of many people who have contributed positively to the history of the British Isles, but it has also spawned a number of people whose outrageous behaviour has provided the media with headlines to titillate or shock the nation.

Some of the people or events may not be regarded as strictly infamous. 'Notorious' might be more appropriate. So, this chapter is devoted to the occasional misdeeds (and worse) of some male Cheshire characters, whose behaviour has upset, shocked, delighted or enthralled the public.

EDWARD HIGGINS

There is little ambiguity about the character of Edward Higgins. He was unquestionably a villain, despite an almost romantic reputation as a gentleman highwayman whose exploits in the early eighteenth century kept the populace enthralled. He was believed to have been born in Worcestershire in about 1726. When he arrived in Knutsford in 1755 Higgins was already on the way to becoming a legend. He had been charged with sheep stealing (a hanging offence), burglary and housebreaking. Fortunately for him he was cleared of sheep stealing, convicted of theft of goods rather than house-breaking and sentenced to be transported to Maryland in America. In typical Higgins fashion he spent barely a month in America. He broke into a house in Boston to steal sufficient cash to pay for his return fare to England.

By the time he arrived in Cheshire he had lived and operated in Worcester, Birmingham, Manchester and Boston. A much-travelled man!

Shortly after arriving in Knutsford his cloak of respectability was enhanced when he married and appeared to settle down in the community. At times he was described as a yeoman, at times as a gentleman, and he also claimed to be a landowner, horse breeder and a seller of farm produce from his own land. He also fathered six children.

On the surface he was comfortably off, a respectable family man and landowner. Who could believe, as he mixed with the local aristocracy, socialised at the hunt, attended horse races and wined and dined with his wealthy neighbours, that he was involved in nefarious activities? By involving himself so closely with his neighbours Higgins was able to identify opportunities for his thieving. He broke into their houses to steal cash, jewellery or gold and would sometimes hold up their carriages in highwayman style when he became aware of their habits and movements. Little did they know that their friendly, sociable neighbour from the big ivy-covered house on Knutsford Heath was abusing their hospitality in the worst possible way. Squire Samuel Egerton, a neighbour and MP for Cheshire who owned Tatton Park, was a personal friend of Higgins.

Higgins stole a very valuable snuff box from Oulton Hall, the home of Philip Egerton, while he was a house guest and in typical detective-story style, Higgins placed himself in charge of the investigation, having first hidden the snuff box in a safe place.

He later admitted to stealing jewellery from a young woman's room in Chester while she lay sleeping. The girl did wake up but believed the shape in the dark was her maid. Higgins confessed years later that if she had challenged him he would have killed her. This admission linked him with the terrible murder in 1764 of a lady and her maid in Bristol. Although Higgins was believed to have been in the area at the time on business, he always strenuously denied being responsible for the brutal slayings. However, it was reported that he told an acquaintance in Knutsford about the Bristol murders during a bout of drinking, long before news could have reached the town, but there was no real proof or evidence to confirm that he was the killer.

Suspicion fell on him in November 1764 after yet another robbery when the parish constables came knocking at the big house on Knutsford Heath. Higgins escaped, made his way to Liverpool and then on to Bristol where he made contact with his wife telling her to sell up in Cheshire.

Once again he bought a large house, and started hunting with horses and hounds and living the life of a country gentleman. His luck almost ran out in February 1767 when he was recognised and arrested on the original charge of having escaped from his deportation sentence. Again the charmed life came into play and he survived a series of court appearances. However, while out on bail he committed a minor robbery in Carmarthenshire leaving behind vital clues which sealed his fate.

He was returned to Worcester to be tried first of all on the deportation charge (despite overwhelming evidence against him and a three-hour trial he was acquitted) and on two minor robbery offences of which he was found guilty and sentenced to death. Higgins's reputation was by now widespread and the courts were packed with people eager to witness his trials and to hear of his exploits.

Higgins was not finished yet and had one more trick up his sleeve. He managed to get a message to his wife to elicit help from well-placed friends. A letter eventually arrived at the prison authorising a stay of execution.

Edward Higgins, gentleman highwayman and villain, lived in this house on Knutsford Heath in the mid-eighteenth century. *(Both images: Bob Burrows)*

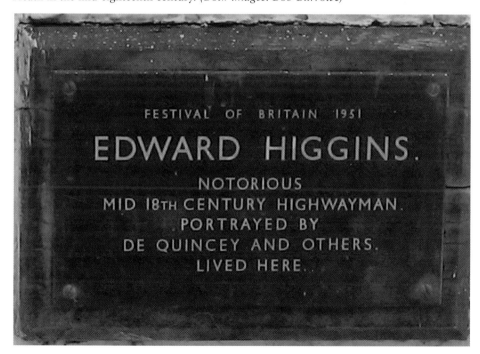

FESTIVAL OF BRITAIN 1951

EDWARD HIGGINS.

NOTORIOUS
MID 18TH CENTURY HIGHWAYMAN.
PORTRAYED BY
DE QUINCEY AND OTHERS.
LIVED HERE.

It looked authentic but was discovered to be a forgery. The game was up. The last throw of the dice had failed. His wife protested to the very end that he was innocent and Higgins also professed his innocence of all charges.

On Saturday 7 November 1767, Edward Higgins, gentleman, landowner, father, socialite, highwayman, thief, liar, scoundrel, killer? was hanged at Pensam near Carmarthen Castle, not far from the scene of his last robbery.

He is still remembered in Knutsford during the annual May Day parade when an 'Edward Higgins' figure walks with other characters in costume through the town. The imposing house in which he once lived still stands overlooking Knutsford Heath and bears a brass plaque recording his name for posterity.

Although the public was intrigued by Higgins's deeds and the charmed life he appeared to live, cocking a snook at authority, he was not the romantic highwayman of Victorian novels. He was a scoundrel and he may well have been a killer. Surely he deserves the epithet 'Infamous'.

THOMAS UNETT BROCKLEHURST

A man who would certainly be unaware that he had committed an act of infamy, the repercussions of which reverberate today, was Thomas Unett Brocklehurst of the famous Brocklehurst silk tycoon family of Macclesfield. Thomas was a much-respected adventurer and explorer who travelled the world during the late nineteenth century. It is Brocklehurst who many believe was responsible for the introduction to Britain of the grey squirrel which he brought back to his Henbury estate, Macclesfield, from America in 1876.

At first considered to be an endearing creature, the grey squirrel is now regarded as vermin and its numbers are virtually out of control. There are more than 2 million grey squirrels in England alone. It is about a third larger than the red squirrel and is more aggressive. There have been reports of attacks by the grey and one particular incident featured in the press was of a grey squirrel which grabbed a setter dog by sinking its teeth into the dog's snout and resisting all attempts to dislodge it. The poor dog was only released on the intervention of a vet. There have been numerous instances of greys defending their young and their territory by adopting threatening postures, growling and rushing at the intruder. Sharp claws, sharp teeth, high speed and great agility make this small creature a formidable foe. In addition the greys destroy nests and eat birds' eggs; they also have a liking for tree bark and by stripping the protective bark from trees they can destroy whole sections of forest. In many places in Britain they have decimated the indigenous red squirrel population by destroying their habitat and passing on the parapox virus that kills the red squirrel within weeks. Red squirrels are now an endangered species.

Grey squirrels are thought to have been introduced to Britain from America by Thomas Unett Brocklehurst of Macclesfield in 1876. *(Bob Burrows)*

A 2005 survey estimated that there were now only about 20,000 red squirrels surviving, mainly in Northumberland, North Yorkshire, parts of Cumbria and in Merseyside. The only surviving colony in the south of England is on the Isle of Wight. They are not aggressive and do little harm to the environment. Their diet is more varied than that of the grey and consists of nuts, flowers, fruit, berries, seeds, and sometimes insects, in their preferred habitat of pine forest. They generally have a more appealing, lovable nature and are considered to be the 'good guys'.

Steps to protect the reds by controlling the greys were announced in November 2005 by Red Alert North England, a group that comprises Wildlife Trusts, the Forestry Commission, landowners and anyone with an interest in conservation and the protection of British wildlife. They are working on establishing a no-go zone for grey squirrels to protect the reds' sixteen strongholds in the north of England. A 3-mile exclusion zone will surround the selected conifer forests and act as a buffer. Grey squirrels will be exterminated by shooting or trapping if they encroach into this area. It is hoped that this will enable the red squirrel to flourish in Sefton Sands, Southport, Widdale near Hawes in Yorkshire, Whinfell, Penrith and Kielder Forest, Northumberland.

Although the strategy has received much support, some organisations, particularly the European Squirrel Initiative Group, believes that the only way to save the red squirrel is by eradicating the greys over a much wider area of England. They have gone so far as to suggest that if the campaign does not become more widespread, the red squirrel will probably die out within twenty years. Thomas Brocklehurst has much to answer for.

CAPTAIN H.C. BROCKLEHURST

Another Brocklehurst family member, Captain H.C. Brocklehurst, earned wide condemnation following his expedition to China in 1935. Brocklehurst shot a giant panda, had it stuffed and brought it back to this country. The panda even then was extremely rare and endangered and people were outraged by his action. At best his behaviour was naïve and certainly crass

Giant panda shot by Capt H.C. Brocklehurst in China, 1935. *(Macclesfield Museum)*

and insensitive. The national newspapers branded his action as 'scandalous'. The panda was believed to have been one of the largest ever shot and was taken to Berlin to be exhibited just before the start of the Second World War. It was believed that Goering was very interested in buying it but Brocklehurst refused all his offers and it was returned to England. The family eventually gave the stuffed panda to Macclesfield West Park Museum where it can still be seen today.

LIEUTENANT-COLONEL SIR WALTER BROMLEY-DAVENPORT

Another man, for whom the epithet 'eccentric' is more appropriate than 'infamous', was Lieutenant-Colonel Sir Walter Bromley-Davenport. It is said that today, British politics is devoid of characters, which is very probably true. Political correctness allows little latitude for personal expression. Today's environment would have little appeal for the flamboyant former Tory MP for Knutsford, Bromley-Davenport.

The Davenports are a long-established Cheshire family who played a prominent part in the county of Cheshire for many years. The family engaged in community, county and national affairs not only from a sense of duty but also from a willingness to serve.

It is widely believed that Sir Walter could have made a greater impact in his political career and advanced to higher office if he had been more compliant and more subservient to his superiors. His only career recognition came with his appointment as junior whip in 1949. Regrettably even this belated acknowledgement of his service lasted no more than two years and ended when he committed an act of infamy, which has passed into parliamentary folklore.

Sir Walter vigourously approached a 'colleague' who was trying to leave the House of Commons before the 10 o'clock voting deadline. Taking a dim view of what he perceived to be an offence, Sir Walter, in perhaps an overzealous attempt to express his displeasure, kicked the man from behind, knocking him down the stairs. To his horror and to that of the other onlookers (and to the delight of many others) the 'colleague' turned out to be the Belgian Ambassador. The story was and is frequently retold.

Although Sir Walter liked to play up to his likeable maverick image, he was no fool. He was a former lightweight Army boxing champion, loved the arts, particularly drama, and even installed a theatre in his magnificent country house, Capesthorne Hall. He was renowned for his loud voice and enjoyed bullying new MPs, particularly Labour MPs. As they nervously stood to make their maiden speech, he would yell in a stentorian voice, 'Take your hands out of your pockets.' Even when one of his colleagues, a brigadier, attempted to speak while Sir Walter was on his feet he bellowed, 'Sit down.'

Capesthorne Hall, near Macclesfield, family home of the eccentric Tory MP Lieutenant-Colonel Sir Walter Bromley-Davenport. *(Bob Burrows)*

On occasion his outrageous behaviour could be extremely irritating. Once he boarded a crowded train at Crewe and started to yell, 'All change, all change', as he walked down the corridor. When the train was sufficiently empty, he selected a good seat for himself and sat down. There is no record of what the other passengers thought

His approach to life and to politics in particular is best illustrated when in 1987 during the general election his successor Neil Hamilton asked him to address a meeting. Just before the meeting Hamilton noticed that Sir Walter had a wad of crumpled, dog-eared, grubby sheets of notes which he was thumbing through. Puzzled and intrigued, Hamilton asked him when he had prepared those notes and was startled when Sir Walter replied, '1945'. He went on to explain that he had prepared the notes after his return from the Second World War and had delivered the same speech from the same notes at every general election for the past forty-two years. No spin-doctors, advisers or speechwriters for him.

HEWLET JOHNSON

Hewlet Johnson, an old boy of King's School, Macclesfield, earned himself political infamy in the late 1940s and early 1950s. Born in Macclesfield in 1874 he left King's School in 1893 and went to Manchester University and thence to Oxford. He started his working life as an apprentice engineer but changed direction after doing welfare work in the Manchester slums. He joined the Labour Party and then devoted his life to the Church.

He became Dean of Manchester and then Canterbury but when he started to become involved in politics, his socialist views and leanings towards communism started to attract hostility.

At a time of 'Cold War' and the perceived threat of communism to the free world, his sympathies, writings and pronouncements on the 'idealistic' way of life in the Soviet Union earned him the wrath of the media and the public in Britain. Many regarded his views as treasonable.

He was mockingly dismissed as the 'Red Dean' by the British public. His views received recognition in certain quarters and it was no surprise when the Soviet Union awarded him the Stalin Peace Prize in 1951, acknowledging his services to their cause. Johnson died in 1966.

DR PETER FORSTER, BISHOP OF CHESTER

More than fifty years later another Cheshire clergyman, the Bishop of Chester, Dr Peter Forster, found himself under the national spotlight following his outspoken views on homosexuals. In November 2003 in an article published in the local newspaper, the *Chester Chronicle*, he stated that he believed that homosexuals should receive medical treatment. He went on to say, 'Some people who are primarily homosexual can reorientate themselves. I would encourage them to consider that as an option, but I would not set myself up as a medical specialist on the subject; that's an area of psychiatric health.'

Dr Forster was responsible for helping to write the Church of England report, *Some Issues in Human Sexuality: A Guide to Debate* and he has been consistently critical about issues of 'immorality' in Britain. He has also spoken out against the ordination of homosexual bishops.

The bishop, a married man with four children, is part of the All Souls Day Group which is against the rush to liberalism in the Church. The group condemns sexual activity outside marriage and was fiercely opposed to the appointment of the openly homosexual American bishop Gene Robinson at New Hampshire. Dr Forster was also one of nine bishops who openly opposed the appointment of Dr Jeffrey John who, although a non-practising homosexual, was offered the post of Bishop of Reading. Dr John later declined the position after realising the strength of the opposition to his appointment.

Dr Forster's view that homosexuals ought to seek medical help caused a storm of controversy with strong views expressed on both sides. After receiving a formal complaint Cheshire police launched an investigation to ascertain whether the bishop's remarks had constituted a criminal offence. The police decided that no offence had been committed but the Chief Constable, Peter Fahy, advised that we should all be aware of the position of minorities in the county and make sure that diversity is celebrated. Democracy is all about freedom of speech and the right to express opinion no matter how controversial.

TIMOTHY MALLET

Another Cheshire man enjoying a different kind of notoriety is Marple's Timothy Mallet. Born in 1955, Timothy became extremely popular on children's television where his zany, madcap, knockabout humour and penchant for horrendously bright colours in shirts and huge coloured spectacles provided him with a distinctive image. His television show *Wacaday* started in 1985 and ran for many years. It was his recording of 'Itsy Bitsy Teeny Weeny Yellow Polka Dot Bikini' which unbelievably went to number one in the UK popular music charts and brought him notoriety. In a Channel 4 television show in January 2004, viewers were invited to vote for the '100 Worst Pop Records' ever made. Timothy Mallet's rendition was voted the thirteenth worst ever record.

FREDDIE STARR

Liverpool-born Freddie Starr spent several of his creative years in Birkenhead trying to break into show business. His career was covered in *Cheshire's Famous* and his talent for impersonation, comedy and music are well known to the British public. Freddie also had a dark side and producers started to avoid him, believing him to be unreliable and unsteady. His slurred speech gave the impression that he was the worse for drink; in fact, as he stated in his autobiography he was hooked on valium. Throughout this low period in his career, Des O'Connor stood by him and invited him onto his show, although he was unsure of just what Starr would do. It made for good television and Starr regained his popularity.

However, the headline in the *Sun* newspaper of 13 March 1986, 'Freddie Starr Ate My Hamster', horrified the British public. Lea La Salle, a 23-year-old model, told the *Sun* that she had met Freddie Starr when she was living with her boyfriend in Birchwood, Cheshire. Starr was staying with them while appearing in a Manchester show. When he returned in the early hours of the morning and asked her to get him some food she refused. She said that he then went into the kitchen and came back with her pet hamster, Supersonic, cushioned between two pieces of bread and in front of her eyes he consumed the lot. Freddie denied it and revealed much later that, yes he had stayed at the house, but it had been seven years previously.

The truth was revealed when show-business agent Max Clifford was asked on a BBC2 chat show if Freddie Starr ever did eat that hamster. Clifford replied smilingly, 'Of course not.' Freddie Starr at the time was about to embark on a UK tour. The story and the huge media reaction guaranteed that Freddie's shows were sold out. It had been a set-up to promote the tour and the most infamous show-business story that year was all a con.

CHRIS EVANS

Another show-business figure who appears to make enemies regularly is Warrington-born Chris Evans whose broadcasting court case is featured in Chapter Six. However, his attitude qualifies him to be entered in this section

Chris Evans, ebullient television presenter. *(Warrington Guardian/Eddie Fuller)*

on characters: talented undoubtedly, shrewd clearly, annoying definitely. He is notorious for the way he has treated his staff and colleagues live on air, the pranks he has played on several of his shows, some very funny, and his binge drinking with cronies.

PETER KENYON

In *Cheshire's Famous*, I included the new Chief Executive of Manchester United, Peter Kenyon, who was born in Stalybridge. Kenyon said that he had achieved his lifetime's ambition and had got the job every Manchester United fan would give anything for; it was a pleasure coming to the office and he couldn't imagine working anywhere else. His appointment was beyond his wildest dreams. The world of soccer, not to mention Manchester United supporters, was shocked beyond belief when in August 2003 Kenyon announced his resignation. In an act of unparalleled soccer infamy, he announced his intention to take up the post of Chief Executive at Stamford Bridge, Chelsea!

Peter Kenyon, former Chief Executive of Manchester United. *(Manchester United)*

PAUL DAVIDSON

A highly successful Cheshire businessman also featured in *Cheshire's Famous* is rapidly turning into a character and, if the financial authorities were to be believed in 2003, an infamous character. Paul Davidson, known as 'The Plumber' because of his invention of a radiator connector which made him a fortune, left school at the age of 16 and worked for Shell as a pipefitter before his invention helped him to establish his listed company Oystertec. Over the years he has bought and sold a number of companies and it was the flotation of a new business, Cyprotex, that thrust him into the headlines. The Financial Services Authority (FSA) launched an investigation into the conditions appertaining to the launch. Davidson placed a spread bet of £5 million to underpin the flotation of Cyprotex in which he had a 35 per cent stake. The bet was of such a size that the spread betting firm City Index had to get it covered, which eventually led to 80 per cent of the shares being placed, effectively guaranteeing a successful launch. The FSA ruled that Davidson had deliberately manipulated the market and was therefore guilty of market abuse. Davidson was fined £750,000 – the first time that the FSA had issued financial penalties for market abuse.

Paul Davidson, who lived in Prestbury at the time with his family, vehemently protested his innocence. In January 2004 Davidson's lawyers launched an appeal against the fine to the Financial Services and Markets Tribunal and further announced that Paul Davidson intended to sue the FSA in a civil claim.

Things started to get worse for Davidson when in March 2004 another action concerning the patent rights on his invention, between himself and Oystertec, which he sold in 2002, caused the judge to freeze Davidson's £80 million assets, allowing him £1,000 per week to live on. Davidson claimed that, as a result, he was having to close down businesses, stop work in several other developments and pull out of a couple of ongoing projects. He later said, 'I am completely broke.'

On 4 November 2004 Davidson was sentenced to three months in prison suspended for twelve months, for contempt of court when failing to appear for a court case regarding the patent dispute with Oystertec. Shortly before Christmas 2004 it was revealed that Davidson had indeed become bankrupt. Creditors queued up as the Trade and Industry Secretary Patricia Hewitt appointed accountants PKF to look into the affairs of 'The Plumber'. At various times his fortune has been estimated at between £65 and £200 million. Ownership of eleven homes, including a mansion in Prestbury and a villa in Marbella complete with two swimming pools and a helicopter pad; a yacht, a private jet, nine cars and a chauffeur-driven Bentley, gave an indication of his extreme wealth.

In May 2006 the 'black hole' into which Davidson's world had disappeared was suddenly bathed with light. The Financial Services and Markets Tribunal adjudged that he and fellow defendant Ashley Tatham, the director at spread betting firm City Index who had been found guilty with him, 'did not create the false and misleading impression', and that they did not 'fail to observe the standard of behaviour reasonably expected of them'.

Tatham's lawyer said in a statement, 'It is outrageous that they have been put through this ordeal and have their lives wrecked.'

A completely exonerated Paul Davidson commented, 'They've ruined my life, taken away my money, my business and my status in the community. My wife has left me. This is a humiliating story. One minute you are in a Bentley, the next minute you are on foot. Everybody points at you.' All the trappings of his previously luxurious lifestyle had gone and he was living with his parents.

The Financial Services Authority seemed unrepentant. It refused to accept responsibility for damages or costs and or even to discuss the issue.

Davidson told a newsgathering, 'This should never have come to a tribunal', and pointed out what a huge waste of money the almost four years it had taken to reach an innocent verdict had been. 'We will be pushing for reckless misfeasance,' he concluded.

A figure in excess of £100 million has been mentioned as compensation for the ruin of his business.

It looks as though the phoenix has risen from the ashes and Davidson says that he has another business deal in the offing.

STEVE BENNETT

Steve Bennett, a businessman from Hyde, is either foolhardy, brave or naïve. Suicidal, eccentric or barmy are other descriptions that have been bandied about by the media. A former Colgate toothpaste technician, Steve runs his own company, Starchaser Industries Ltd, and is dedicated to becoming the first man to travel into space in a privately owned spacecraft, thereby claiming a £6 million prize.

The X Prize is offered by a consortium of American businessmen to the first non-government-backed agency to launch humans into space. The space ship must contain three people and transport them to 62 miles above the earth and return twice within a fortnight. In effect, it will be the first privately funded commercial space flight.

Steve has built a capsule with the financial backing of two investors who paid £500,000 on condition that they accompanied him on his epic maiden space voyage taking off from Woomera, Australia, in 2004. One attempt in 1998 attracted the description 'suicidal'. Steve's unmanned *Starchaser 3* rocket was launched on Dartmoor, but travelled very briefly before careering off course and crashing to the ground. The rocket *Thunderbird* which he has invented and hopes will eventually take him into space, is 85ft long. The tiny, single-seater capsule, measuring 9ft long and 3ft wide, underwent landing tests in Florida in 2004. It was pushed manually out of the back of a plane at 13,000ft, descending at 200mph, before three parachutes were activated to effect a landing.

Steve dismisses claims that his attempt is eccentric or bizarre and shrugs off the various warnings, particularly after the destruction of the American spacecraft *Columbia* and its crew. He said that that disaster was caused by human error and his team were well aware of the dangers of complacency. The last stage of his preparation he said was a very personal one: he needed to shed 2st in weight in order to attain greater efficiency. Despite his confidence in his own team he knows that the competition is severe. In June 2004 an American consortium led by Burt Rutan had a first successful flight into space with their *Spaceship One* and became favourites to take the prize.

Undaunted, Steve Bennett was quoted as saying, 'Ours is a better design. But it boils down to the old thing, no bucks, no Buck Rogers. Rutan was given $20 million to win a $10 million prize. That's the way the Americans do things. I haven't got any sour grapes about it. Good luck to the fella – he's worked bloody hard.' Rutan's consortium won the X Prize; Steve did not achieve his dream, but he is still in one piece.

MR METHANE

A man with a truly unique talent can loosely be described as infamous. He makes a living out of a bodily function, which we are all familiar with and yet which many of us would prefer not to advertise, and certainly not rejoice in. The man is known as Mr Methane.

Mr Methane discovered his talent for 'breaking wind' or, to use the blunter expression, 'farting', at the age of 15. He demonstrated his skill in exchange for cash in the playground of the school he attended, Ryles Park County High School, Macclesfield. He only rediscovered his talent when he broke wind (one could say as a moment of light relief) during a boring course he attended while working for British Rail. The gathering was most impressed and, during his time at Macclesfield Station and other postings he was frequently asked to demonstrate his skill. It was another Macclesfield man, Paul Genders, who used to play with the Macclesfield group Screaming Beavers, who persuaded Mr Methane to perform at a local club. Since that historic moment Mr Methane has never looked back.

Dressed in a green, caped crusader, Batman-type outfit and mask and advertising himself as a flatulist, Mr Methane burst upon the world of show business like a breath of fresh air. Well, no, actually, not as a breath of fresh air, but you get the meaning. His art or craft, or whatever one calls it, offers

wonderful opportunities for puns and this is where this chapter descends into tasteless, schoolboy humour. Mr Methane has an incredible array of 'turns' during his stage act, from candle snuffing, dart farting, blowing clouds of talcum powder and performing a whole range of tunes. At this point readers, you may wonder just what his musical tastes are and may want to suggest your own song titles. It's good fun. Here's a sample of my own: 'The Restless Wind', 'Blowing in the Wind', 'Dancing Cheek to Cheek', 'Analweiss' from *The Sound of Music* and 'Trumpet Voluntary'. See, it's easy if you are prepared to lower yourself and indulge. He has a range of nineteen tunes which he can play, as he says, on his 'Anal Organ'.

Mr Methane has found a niche for himself in the market, is in demand for live shows, has appeared on many television programmes, has published a book, an album (no pun intended) and a number of videos in which he performs a range of activities as well as demonstrating his musical repertoire. He is probably the world's only flatulist artist and his fans include Howard Stern, Ali G and Kelsey Grammer (Frasier). Let us hope that the bottom doesn't drop out of his world.

Above: Mr Methane, renowned flatulist, on stage. *(Mr Methane)*

Opposite: Mr Methane demonstrates his talent for breaking wind. *(Mr Methane)*

5

INFAMOUS CHARACTERS: WOMEN

Similarly to the previous chapter on infamous Cheshire men, the women featured here may not be strictly 'infamous', but one thing that they have in common is that they are all strong characters who have caused controversy. These are women with forceful opinions, who are not averse to asserting themselves and certainly do not believe in the old adage that it's a man's world. Oh no. If we also consider Mary Fitton, handmaiden to Elizabeth I, Lady Hamilton and the female regiment which fought in the Civil War, all of whom are featured in Chapter One, then it can be safely ascertained that over the centuries Cheshire has produced some formidable women.

MOTHER REDCAP

A person not mentioned in Chapter One was Mother Redcap, a Wallasey innkeeper living in the late eighteenth to early nineteenth centuries. She was undoubtedly notorious in her time, but was never found guilty of any crime. Known as Mother Redcap because she wore a red hood, she was also described as the wreckers' and smugglers' friend.

Old records have never confirmed the woman's identity, although some historians have suggested the name of Poll Jones. It is believed that the inn was called Mother Redcap because Poll Jones wore a red cap. Situated on the shore near Seacombe with Liscard Moor providing a desolate and forbidding backcloth, the inn was reputed to be involved in the terrible trade of wrecking. The Wirral coastline and the Mersey estuary can be a treacherous region for vessels seeking a safe haven, particularly on a stormy night. Wreckers used to patrol the rocks carrying lanterns. Ships, seeing a light and believing that it was a lighthouse, indicating safety, would head for the beam and be terrified to find that their ship was about to be dashed to pieces on the rocks and their cargo and in many cases their lives lost. Many a sailor, having survived the nightmare of the wreck and battled ashore, would then find himself faced by a gang of wreckers who lost no time in murdering him and making off with cargoes of whisky, silk, tobacco, rum, sugar and whatever else could be got ashore. Smuggling was also a major business for this small neighbourhood and sometimes involved the whole community.

Mother Redcap and her inn were at the centre of this trade. Goods would be taken to the inn and hidden until they could be sold and moved on. A flagpole at the front of the inn had a weather vane in the form of a cock which could be turned to signal if customs officers were in the vicinity. Furthermore, if the heavy-studded front door was forced open, it triggered a device that caused the floorboards behind the door to swivel and open. Any intruder would then fall into the cellar. The ground under the inn and the immediate vicinity was said to be a catacomb of cellars and tunnels in which contraband and men were often hidden. Local men sometimes sought sanctuary there from the marauding press gangs that would seek out, beat and force able-bodied men into service in the Navy.

There are many stories of Mother Redcap's tactics at evading capture; even suggestions that she was the 'brains' behind the operation. The proximity of the inn to the sea and the prosperity of the local people must have made the customs men suspicious. On one occasion a cargo of rich silk had been either salvaged or smuggled and the local women were later seen walking around in dresses of high-quality material. But Mother Redcap was never arrested. The customs men often drank at the inn and no doubt she was a generous hostess which may have resulted in a policy of 'turning a blind eye'.

The story certainly has all the ingredients for a first-class film. One can imagine the inn lit up on a stormy night with the waves crashing on the shore line and the wind whistling across the moors while inside the atmosphere is full of noise and intrigue. Smugglers and wreckers drinking, singing, fighting and arguing among themselves, sometimes in the presence of customs men. The air full of smoke and the curses of hard, weatherbeaten men struggling to survive.

Intriguingly, Mother Redcap was throughout her life entrusted with holding cash and valuable goods for her clients, from whom she took a profit, and because she died suddenly it is not known whether she ever disclosed the whereabouts of her hidden treasure or even if it has ever been discovered. It was known that shortly before her death she concluded a highly profitable cash deal which she probably never had the opportunity to dispose of. So where is it? Perhaps in the catacombs that were said to extend for a considerable distance underneath the inn and beyond, even reaching down to the shore.

The inn survived for some time after the death of Mother Redcap and was bought in 1888 by a wealthy Warrington solicitor who superbly converted the old building into a house. Then it became a café before being demolished in the 1970s with scant regard for its history.

MARY WHITEHOUSE

The first of a trio of formidable Cheshire women is Mary Whitehouse, who was born in Nuneaton but raised in Cheshire. She was educated at Chester Grammar School and then Cheshire County Training College. As a young girl she played tennis for Cheshire and it was said had every prospect of becoming a professional but gave it up to become a teacher.

It was in the Swinging Sixties when liberalism and sexual freedom, particularly among the young, erupted in Britain, that she became the self-appointed guardian of British morals, the founder and President of the National Viewers' and Listeners' Association. At first her campaign was regarded by the vast majority as justifiable as the public was being exposed to strong language, nudity and violence on television, seemingly without any form of censorship. But it became clear that she had a zero tolerance for what many believed was a maturing adult generation who were perfectly able to judge between good and bad and right and wrong.

Her crusade, for that is what it became, had her travelling the length and breadth of the UK railing against the 'tide of filth' threatening to engulf our society. Many believed that she was taking her role as crusader too seriously when she started to criticise inoffensive swear words and to object to the tone of several highly popular television programmes of the era. For example, she found the use of the word 'bum' offensive and said that it must always be 'bottom'. She objected to the *Benny Hill Show* for its basic humour and she found the Alf Garnett show, *Till Death Us Do Part* and the ground-breaking, satirical *That Was The Week That Was* unacceptable, and yet all three programmes were the most popular in Britain. Who was out of touch? Mary Whitehouse or the British public? Her views were repeated time and again in a headmistressy tone, she was uncompromising, outspoken, and fast becoming a cult figure and a target for ridicule. Comedians told jokes about her, impressionists mimicked her and one magazine publisher specialising in nude ladies changed the name of the magazine to *Whitehouse*.

Despite the backlash, her efforts to protect and safeguard the morals of the nation were acknowledged when she was awarded the CBE in 1980. Mary Whitehouse, raised in Cheshire, self-appointed protector of the nation's morals, died aged 91 in 2001. She perhaps did not make Britain a better place in which to live but for a time she certainly made it more interesting.

CHRISTINE HAMILTON

Another formidable woman who has become a regular performer in the media arena is Christine Hamilton. Christine has, as the wife of former disgraced Conservative MP for Tatton, Neil Hamilton, lived in Cheshire for more than

Former MP Neil Hamilton and his formidable wife Christine. *(Knutsford Guardian)*

twenty years. She met Neil Hamilton in the House of Commons where she worked as secretary to Sir Gerald Nabarro, and then for seventeen years she was secretary to her husband until he left the House of Commons in 1997.

During the trials and tribulations endured by the couple over the years she has been a formidable fighter on behalf of her husband and her tenacity has often caused hardened journalists to quake in their boots. In a face-to-face encounter with her husband's opponent, the Independent candidate Martin Bell (see page 67), the attending media circus acknowledged that she got the better of him. She later described Bell as, 'ghastly and sanctimonious in his pinny-white suit'. Loud and voluble, she handled the media with a firmness which earned her the nickname 'Battleaxe'. Undaunted, she chose the music 'Ride of The Valkyries' as the call tone on her mobile phone and wrote a book entitled *Christine Hamilton's Bumper Book of British Battleaxes* which was published in 1997.

Her high profile helped the Hamiltons to generate much-needed income to meet the crippling costs of their unsuccessful action against Mohamed Al Fayed, whom she memorably dismissed as a 'Ghastly little Egyptian grocer on Brompton Road'. To the media she was a godsend and was at times mercilessly ridiculed on satirical television and radio shows. Battleaxe, Lioness, Wife From Hell, She Who Must Be Obeyed, were just some of the nicknames bestowed on her.

Largely through her efforts, the Hamiltons were much in demand and appeared on a wide range of programmes. Christine was a guest on *Have I Got News For You, Any Questions, Newsnight* and had her own show, *Choice*, on the BBC, and became the presenter on the Sky financial programme, *Simply Money.*

The public's perception of her gradually changed and became more understanding when her softer, more vulnerable side was revealed on several occasions. In the popular television show *I'm A Celebrity Get Me Out Of Here*, her caring attitude for the others and the way in which she faced a tirade of abuse from boxer Nigel Benn earned respect. Her genuine tears during an appearance on *Who Wants To Be A Millionaire* for failing to earn sufficient money for her charity endeared her to the public. The battleaxe had a soft side.

During the filming of the Louis Theroux show, the Hamiltons were arrested by the police on allegations that they had been involved in the rape of a young woman. They received much public support for the dignified way in which they handled their arrest on charges which were later proven to be not only spurious, but disgracefully so.

The Hamiltons must now be respected for the way in which they have fought to rebuild their lives and to meet their commitments after the 'cash for questions' scandal, which all but destroyed them. They still claim that they are innocent of the allegations made against them by Al-Fayed. If that is the case, then the Hamiltons are the victims of a truly infamous injustice.

In 2003 they finally sold their much-loved home in Alderley Edge, Cheshire, and moved to London to be closer to the work environment in which they now operate. Television, radio, newspapers, even pantomime and after-dinner speaking by both of them have opened up new avenues.

The late journalist Lynda Lee Potter perhaps best summed up Christine Hamilton: 'She has the valour of the early Christian martyrs. With more women like her Britain would never have lost the Empire.'

ANN WINTERTON

Another feisty lady unafraid to speak her mind which serves her well, for most of the time, in her chosen field of politics, is Ann Winterton. Born in 1941, Lady Winterton does not originate from Cheshire but has been associated with the county since her husband, Sir Nicholas Winterton,

Ann Winterton, MP, whose ill-judged jokes caused a storm of criticism. *(Brian Ollier)*

became Conservative MP for Macclesfield in 1971. After supporting her husband and raising four children, she decided she would like to enter the world of politics in her own right and in 1983 became Member of Parliament for Congleton, the constituency in which the Wintertons live.

Hard-working and popular with her constituents, Ann's ability was acknowledged by the Conservative hierarchy with a series of appointments: chairman of the All Party Pro Life GP 1991, Chairman's Panel 1992–8, Opposition Frontbench Spokesman on National Drugs Strategy 1998–2001, culminating in her appointment as Shadow Minister for Agriculture and Fisheries 2001–2. Ann Winterton was seen as a rising star with potential for higher office.

However, her career started to unravel when in 2002 she told what many people thought was a racist joke at a rugby club dinner in her constituency. The joke finished with the punchline, 'The Englishman threw the Pakistani out [of a train window], saying they're ten-a-penny in my country.' It was of course leaked to the press and caused a storm. Ann protested long and hard that her comments were not racist and had been taken out of context. Despite her protests she was forced into making an apology and the then Tory leader Ian Duncan Smith decided that he had little option other than to sack her. She lost her post as Shadow Minister and settled down to represent her constituents away from the public glare and controversy.

In *Cheshire's Famous* I said that I was certain that Ann Winterton would not be phased by the setback to her career and 'would continue to speak her mind'. How prophetic my comment. In February 2004 she created an even greater storm with another joke. *The Daily Mirror* screamed out 'TORY MP'S RACIST JOKE ON COCKLERS'. Lady Winterton had struck again. More than twenty Chinese illegal immigrant cocklers had been drowned in a terrible tragedy in Morecambe Bay. The papers alleged that Ann Winterton had attended a dinner in Westminster designed to improve Anglo-Danish relations, to which figures from industry and other MPs had been invited. Ann Winterton's leaked joke was reported as concerning two sharks swimming in the Atlantic and one turns to the other and says, 'I'm fed up with chasing tuna. Why don't we go to Morecambe Bay and get some Chinese?'

Reports stated that the joke was received in stony silence by the guests who regarded her comments as grossly offensive. The Labour Party was delighted at the 'gaff' because new Tory leader Michael Howard had made a point of deploring racism as a matter of policy.

He was forced to sack her when she refused to apologise for her comments, which she said were not as reported and were made at a private dinner. She further questioned the restriction on freedom of speech if private conversations were to be reported and personal opinions were not respected. She did, of course, deplore the tragic deaths of the Chinese cocklers, but insisted that the 'joke' had been reported out of context. It was at best totally naïve and at worst a gross misjudgement because she insists that she is not a racist.

A torrent of criticism descended on her from all quarters. The Conservative Party withdrew the party whip, local Congleton constituency officials threatened her with de-selection after condemning her behaviour, and one newspaper described her as 'the idiot Tory MP who can't stop telling her racist jokes'. Dr Peter Kolker, chairman of the Congleton Conservative Association, was reported as saying, 'She has let herself down very badly and she ought to apologise to the Chinese community and to all the people she offended.' The Tory leader of Congleton Borough Council commented, 'The first joke she made two years ago was tasteless and offensive, but this one is just sick.' He went on to say that she should have learned from the last time and that she had made a grave error.

Although the whip was withdrawn by the Conservative Party and she was not allowed to take her place in the House of Commons, the decision of whether she remains Conservative MP for Congleton lies with the local constituency. Shortly after the storm she did attend Parliament, but sat with the Ulster Unionists and issued a statement in which she said that the removal of the whip 'will not impact on my ability or determination to represent my constituents'.

Several weeks after the incident, when all parties had had time to reconsider, Ann Winterton issued a full apology to Michael Howard, the then Tory party leader, making it clear that her remarks had been taken out of context and that she believed that she was the victim of 'political correctness'. She said, 'I apologise unreservedly for repeating in private conversation an offensive e-mail circulating on the web.' She also apologised to the Chinese community for unintentionally causing them offence. The Tory party accepted her apology and the party whip was restored, enabling her to assume her parliamentary duties.

DEE CATTON

Britain's most infamous devotee of plastic surgery is Cheshire resident Dee Catton. It is believed that over the years Dee has spent more than £40,000 on various enhancements to her appearance. Stomach, face and breasts have all received the benefits of plastic surgery.

At one time Dee admitted that she was addicted to plastic surgery and her notoriety had led to her being featured in many a television programme, as well as magazine and newspaper articles. She also had a role in the television documentary series *Cheshire Sex*, in which she lifted the lid on the sexual proclivities of the Cheshire set.

Dee lived for a number of years in Wilmslow, but after her divorce she moved to Langley near Macclesfield in 2003. She was particularly scathing of Wilmslow saying that the majority of the populace were too snobbish and arrogant. It didn't help that some of the Wilmslow residents objected to the comments she made on *Cheshire Sex* which ultimately contributed to her decision to leave the town.

Dee has certainly had a colourful career to date. As well as her television work she had a spell as a topless barmaid in Alderley Edge and had an unsuccessful attempt at being a pop star. She could be seen driving around the Cheshire area in her highly distinctive canary yellow Lotus with her personal number plate, SIII EXY, in search of employment opportunities.

SARAH HARDING

A young Cheshire woman, very much a girl of today, is Poynton's pop star Sarah Harding. Sarah very courageously confessed to a national newspaper in December 2003 of a period in her young life of which she is not particularly proud.

Sarah came to fame when she survived the gruelling ordeal of selection by the public following a series of television auditions on ITV's *Popstars: The Rivals* to find a five-girl pop band. It had a huge audience and Sarah's group, Girls Aloud, had a UK number one hit with their first single, 'Sounds of the Underground', at Christmas 2002 and followed that with the record 'Jump', which reached number two in the charts.

They were groomed and promoted as successors to the Spice Girls and their management were conscious of the need to project a squeaky-clean image for the benefit of their many young fans. The group suffered a knock when band member Cheryl Tweedy was convicted in 2003 of assaulting a female toilet attendant.

Sarah's bravery in admitting that as a 16-year-old she had started to take cannabis at a low point in her life, had a positive purpose. She confessed that she had smoked cannabis at a party when she was depressed and vulnerable following the break-up of her parents' marriage. It was also a time when she was trying to get into show-business and felt the pain of rejection and frustration. Stand-by jobs, such as barmaid, waitressing, singing in pubs and clubs around Cheshire and handing out leaflets for nightclubs such as Volts in Stockport, fell far short of what she felt her talents deserved. Like many others, she sought comfort in drugs and for about two years, until the age of 18, cannabis helped blot out the reality of her day-to-day existence. Significantly she said that during her drug-taking days she never actually bought any drugs herself, although the habit was widespread in her circle of friends.

Sarah Harding of the pop group Girls Aloud. *(Stockport Express)*

Sarah revealed that she was happy to admit to this negative period in her life as she hoped that it would act as an example not to be followed, not only by the fans of Girls Aloud but by all young people. She clearly believed in herself enough to give it up and one day just decided to stop. Her confessional finished with a positive message when she said that she believed that the use of soft drugs does lead to the taking of hard drugs. Her habit had not graduated to the taking of ecstasy, cocaine or speed but that could have been a natural progression to the next stage and oblivion.

Sarah said, 'Drugs aren't big and they're not clever', and went on to emphasise, 'No matter what happens in your life, turning to drugs won't help. You should talk to someone. Things are never so bad that you have to do something that will harm your body.'

It looks as if Sarah's dark days are gone and at the tender age of 24 she is a successful singer with a great future ahead of her. Her courage in admitting her shortcomings and the lessons learned in her teenage years will hopefully stand her in good stead in the years to come.

6

COURT CASES
AND TRIALS

In recent times Cheshire-born citizens and Cheshire residents have committed or had committed against them acts of infamy which have featured in television programmes and captured the attention of the tabloids and broadsheets.

Incredibly, Cestrians have played a part in the biggest royal family scandal, Britain's greatest financial fraud, the most disgraceful police inquiry, Parliament's longest-running sleaze scandal, an international murder trial, one of show-business's most expensive law cases and an abduction.

BARLOW CLOWES

Lancashire-born Peter Clowes was the perpetrator in the 1980s of Britain's greatest ever financial fraud. Through his company Barlow Clowes he defrauded an estimated 18,000 clients, mainly small investors who lost their life savings after being promised a safe haven. When the company collapsed in 1988 owing £190 million, a number of the cheated clients, their life savings gone, committed suicide.

Born in Flixton in 1942, Clowes was educated at Chorlton Grammar School and went to work at his father's hardware store in Moss Side, Manchester. After the family moved to Heaton Moor he remained in the family business until his father retired. At the age of 21 he married and started out on his business career by setting up a landscaping and turf supply company based in Poynton. The business did well and he was able to buy his first house, a cottage in Marple.

Shortly afterwards he met Elizabeth Barlow who impressed him not only with her looks but also with her sharpness and vitality. It was she who persuaded him to enter the world of finance and he joined her as an insurance salesman at International Life Insurance Company in 1970. At this time Peter Clowes was not yet regarded as a gifted salesman and when he and Elizabeth worked for Cannon in Manchester his role changed to that of network coordinator for intermediaries dealing with the company. She was bright, clever and persuasive whereas Clowes came across as pompous and arrogant, qualities which did not endear him to clients or colleagues. It was while they were working for Cannon that they decided to set up in business for themselves and form Barlow Clowes, a name which would reverberate around the world.

The business did well monitoring guaranteed income bonds for professional business people with Clowes controlling the administrative side. Domestic upheaval followed Clowes's affair with Elizabeth Barlow and his marriage broke up in 1978. He bought his wife a house and for a time he lived in a flat in Heaton Mersey. The house in Marple was renovated and put on the market and during a flurry of property deals he bought his parents a house in Stockport.

A change of direction in his highly successful business was inevitable as he wanted to control other people's money and he diversified into government investments: gilts. Very soon growth necessitated larger premises and more staff. It was during this time that he employed a telephonist, Pamela Haydock who would become his second wife. Part of the success of this phase in his business was down to advertising and to on-the-road financial seminars at places like the Belgrade Hotel, Stockport. But the nature of his methods was starting to unravel.

During his gilt dealings on behalf of his clients he would also keep the best deal for himself. He had set up a secret facility in Jersey which enabled him to move funds around whenever necessary. It was during this period that his affair with Elizabeth Barlow ended and she returned to work for Cannon. A warrant was issued for her arrest following investigations into transactions in her own name, but before she could be apprehended she fled the country. Although Elizabeth Barlow and several of their colleagues were being investigated, Clowes was not. The Department of Trade and Industry was aware in 1981 that Barlow Clowes was trading without a licence but took no action other than to 'monitor' the situation. In 1982 another golden opportunity was presented to Peter Clowes. The BBC's much-respected financial programme, *Money Box*, invited him to appear to comment on the system and principle of bond washing. This was a method of manipulating the buying and selling of gilts to enable the dividend to be taxable as a capital gain rather than the more punishing dividend. Clowes came across very well, stressing that there was absolutely no risk to capital and, unsurprisingly, attracted a massive national interest. He expanded his London office and rapidly moved from small company status into the big boys' league. Crucially, he was still unlicensed.

The year 1982 was a good one. He married Pamela Haydock, having divorced his first wife in 1979, and they moved into Swingate Cottage, Whitley Green, near Macclesfield, which featured an indoor swimming pool, stables, huge gardens and six bedrooms. Palatial indeed. It would be revealed later that this 1772 property was bought with his clients' monies held in Jersey. Life for Clowes could not be better. Weekdays were spent in his

Peter Clowes, the subject of Britain's biggest fraud trial, 1991. *(Manchester Evening News)*

London office and weekends in Macclesfield where he attended dinner parties and the social round.

Storm clouds were gathering. The Jersey authorities wanted Barlow Clowes off the island; several of the British newspapers, uncomfortable with his methods, refused to advertise his products and the DTI was also hovering in the background. Anticipating further trouble, Clowes opened an office in Geneva. He continued in business and in 1984 was forced to apply for a licence. Incredibly, he managed to talk his way out of a tight situation and he survived. His business continued to thrive and money poured in from unsuspecting investors amounting to several millions a week. Clowes bought an office block: Queensway House in Poynton.

The DTI was unhappy about his operation and at one stage contemplated closing Barlow Clowes down. Peter Hayes, a Macclesfield investment adviser, had been pressing the DTI to take action against Barlow Clowes and had passed on his concerns to Macclesfield MP, Nicholas Winterton, who alerted the Minister for Consumer and Corporate Affairs. The combined pressure finally forced the DTI, the Treasury and the Bank of England to take steps to clean up Barlow Clowes and place it on a more legal footing. They also wanted to avoid provoking a major financial scandal by closing down the business with the resulting huge losses.

Their enquiries and investigations did not reveal any serious discrepancies in the company's books. Clowes had simply covered shortfalls by switching funds from the off-shore account, the existence of which the inspectors had not discovered during their investigations. Despite all the searches Barlow Clowes was now licensed and deemed to be legitimate. Peter Clowes had a licence to continue defrauding his unfortunate clients. The millions flowed into his coffers and flowed out again for his private use.

In September 1986 more than 150 guests, including Robert Maxwell, attended the opening of Barlow Clowes International Head Office in Gibraltar. A private jet flew some of the guests to the lavish event, which was attended by a number of government ministers. Clowes's personal self-indulgence had reached staggering levels. At various times he owned a château in Switzerland, a penthouse in Marbella, the large house in Macclesfield now with helicopter pad, a 75ft speedboat, a yacht formerly owned by Tina Onassis, a private plane, a farm in Surrey and a jewellery business. The trappings of his lifestyle included travelling regularly to his various properties and businesses by privately hired Lear jets.

However, his luck could not last for ever and finally the clamour for action led the DTI to move once again into his organisation early in 1988. The inspectors moved into his Poynton Head Office, but Clowes and his team had already started a massive shredding operation. Indeed a team hand-picked by Clowes had been sent out to Gibraltar specifically to amend and shred any compromising evidence. Despite this, sufficient

Prestbury village centre where Peter Clowes was arrested in 1988. *(Bob Burrows)*

evidence was found to justify an arrest and the business was closed down on 27 May 1988.

On a quiet Wednesday morning, 15 June 1988, Peter Clowes was dramatically arrested. A police team waited for him to drive into Prestbury village to collect his morning paper. As his car approached the village church, Clowes was pulled over, arrested and taken to Macclesfield Police Station. Britain's biggest-ever fraud trial commenced on 2 July 1991. Just three years after the closure of Barlow Clowes, Peter Clowes was charged with theft, conspiring to deceive, making false statements to get people to invest with him and a variety of other charges. He was found guilty on eighteen of the nineteen charges and the judge described the case as the very worst of frauds and sentenced him to the maximum term allowed, ten years in prison.

It is estimated that over £90 million owed to small investors, the retired and those who were saving for retirement had been squandered by Clowes's greed and dishonesty. He had gambled with people's life savings and had caused great upset and anxiety to those whose lives had been destroyed as a result.

THE STALKER AFFAIR

The 1980s saw another very high-profile investigation involving Cheshire resident John Stalker, who was Deputy Chief Constable of the Greater Manchester police force. Stalker was the victim of an infamous act.

In May 1984 he was appointed to investigate allegations that the Royal Ulster Constabulary had instigated an unofficial 'shoot-to-kill' policy in its dealings with the IRA. When it became clear that his inquiry was on the verge of revealing information that would be highly sensitive and embarrassing to the authorities, he was suddenly suspended pending investigations into allegations of his own misconduct. The blatant attempt to smear John Stalker and to tarnish his hitherto unblemished police record was a clumsy and infamous attempt to discredit his reputation purely because his own professionalism and tenacity was bringing him close to the truth and would perhaps embarrass and compromise officials at the highest level.

Born in Manchester in 1939, John Stalker became a police cadet in 1956 and rose rapidly through the ranks including experience as a Manchester Detective Sergeant working on the Moors Murders case. In 1978 he became the youngest Detective Chief Superintendent and his career to date had included time served in the Serious Crime Squad, Drug Squad and Bomb Squad. In 1984 following four years as Assistant Chief Constable, he was promoted to the much coveted post of Deputy Chief Constable of Greater Manchester police, the largest provincial police force in the country.

Clearly a man of great ability, his talents had been recognised at various levels by a variety of judges. His duties in Manchester had enabled him to gain further experience and to visit other countries to share expertise and learn how to cope with terrorism and international crime.

Stalker was a talented man at the height of his abilities and respected by all. It came as no great surprise when in 1984 he was appointed to head an inquiry into the murder of six IRA men who had been shot dead in 1982 without, it was alleged, being first given the opportunity to surrender.

Initially the investigations had been requested and authorised by the Chief Constable of the RUC. As Stalker and his team became more and more persistent in their questioning, the RUC at all levels, from the top down, became obstructive and uncooperative. Records of interviews, audiotapes of conversations and files were requested and, after passing through various levels of officialdom, were usually refused. It became a traumatic time for John Stalker with his team being obstructed at all levels and terrorist groups threatening to kill him. Nevertheless he battled on until his legs were kicked from under him – not by the enemy but by his own side.

In early 1986 he felt that he had sufficient evidence to confront the RUC and to demand responses. He said later that although there were no written instructions, nothing pinned on the notice board, he believed that there was a clear understanding on the part of the men whose job it was to pull the trigger that that was what was expected of them. In other words that there was an unofficial 'shoot-to-kill' policy. His findings if made public would have created a massive political explosion in Northern Ireland.

Dark clouds were starting to gather in Stalker's sky. Warning bells rang when he discovered that a secret police unit had been established to investigate a police officer. Earlier, a long-standing friend of his, Manchester businessman Kevin Taylor, had been investigated despite police assurances to Stalker that he had not been targeted. In May 1986 Taylor's offices and his private house were visited and searched by Manchester CID and Stalker's attempts to find out why fell on stony ground. Events quickly and bizarrely came to a head.

On the night of 27 May, John Stalker dined with his boss and representatives of BBC television. The evening passed amicably with no hint or indication of the bombshell to follow. The following day Stalker was called to a meeting with his boss and was promptly suspended while an investigation was held into 'disciplinary offences'. The offences were later alleged to include having undesirable associations with known criminals and enjoying their lavish hospitality. On 29 May the real reason for these 'trumped-up charges' was revealed when he was informed that he was being removed permanently from the Northern Ireland investigation and in the meantime, while further investigations were pursued, he was to remain at home.

The desperation and pettiness of the smear campaign became all too clear when he was asked about his use of police cars, his attendance at Kevin Taylor's birthday party five years previously, his attendance at an Autumn Ball where he was seen to be talking to Taylor and allegations that Taylor had paid for Stalker's air fares on a holiday in America. Later Stalker proved that they had paid their own air fares and use of police cars was found to be well within the police regulations. As the investigations became more petty and invasive the strain on the Stalker family was horrendous and at times unbearable. John Stalker recalled in his excellent book, *Stalker*, the utter humiliation he felt when Stella, his wife for almost twenty-five years, had to produce details of all the family's personal savings accounts, credit card transactions and detail virtually every item of income and expenditure

John Stalker, former Deputy Chief Constable of the Greater Manchester police force. *(Bob Burrows)*

including household and holiday spending. However, the Stalkers also received considerable support from a variety of sources.

Holed up in their Cheshire smallholding in Dunham Massey, the family was besieged by the media. Newpaper, television and radio reporters, who were largely supportive, camped on their doorstep eager for news and interviews. The national press was of the opinion that John Stalker was being stitched up and questions were also raised in the House of Commons. It appeared obvious to all but the police authorities that the allegations against Stalker were groundless.

With regard to his personal integrity no wrongdoing of any kind was found and the allegations that some of his friends had been involved in criminal activities amounted laughingly to minor misdemeanours such as traffic offences or parking tickets. On 22 August, after a period of silence the Police Committee unanimously cleared John Stalker of all charges and he was reinstated as Deputy Chief Constable. However, there were still a number of hurdles to jump and questions to answer.

Stalker's return to work was uncomfortable and made more difficult when he was presented with a bill for £22,000 to cover the costs of defending himself against the various spurious charges. The bill was sufficient to financially cripple the Stalkers and when the Police Committee refused to assist with the payment they were faced with having to sell their Cheshire home. However, the newspapers and the public rallied round to correct what everyone perceived to be an injustice and donations poured into a fighting fund to help pay the bill. At this point the Chief Constable stepped in and threatened Stalker with disciplinary action if he accepted the donations. The Home Office ruled on appeal that they had no objections to the public fund if the Police Committee approved. The Police Committee said in turn that they had no objections if the Association of Chief Police Officers (ACPO) approved. The ACPO said no, the public donations were unacceptable. The President of the ACPO happened to be James Anderton, Stalker's boss. It was the Police Committee which eventually relented and the public donations once again flooded in and the very grateful Stalker family were able to pay the legal fees.

John Stalker continued as Deputy, but understandably the relationship started to deteriorate. In March 1987 Stalker deemed that his own position was untenable and he walked away from the force, which he had served loyally for thirty years.

The case which had dominated the national headlines for months almost destroyed John Stalker. He survived because he had the strength and support of a loyal and loving family. He also received enormous encouragement from a staggering 15,000-plus letters of support from the British public who believed that he was a decent and honest man.

Perhaps at this point I should throw my hat in the ring. Towards the end of the 1980s and during the early 1990s I had the pleasure of knowing John and Stella Stalker on a personal level. It was quite clear to me that he was an intelligent, warm, likeable man whose integrity and honesty I would never doubt. What happened to him and his family was not only infamous but it was a national disgrace. His only crime was to accept a position of great sensitivity and responsibility and to pursue his brief honestly and profession- ally. His reward had almost been personal and professional destruction.

What became of the Northern Ireland investigations that had been handed over to Chief Constable Colin Sampson of the West Yorkshire force? Eventually a diluted version of Stalker's report was published, identifying a number of RUC personnel and suggesting that prosecutions be made. However, in the interests of national security (a convenient blanket), it was decided that no prosecutions should be made.

What of John Stalker? Well there was plenty of life left in the 47-year-old after his resignation in 1987. His first job back in 'civvy street' was as General Manager of Channel 4 TV, responsible for the Liverpool soap *Brookside*. After just a few months in the post he resigned to write his account of the extraordinary events which had befallen him. The book, *Stalker* became a worldwide bestseller and went some way to satisfying his earlier ambition to enter journalism. He moved on to become a respected feature writer for a variety of newspapers and magazines, had a spell as a television presenter, became a commentator and consultant for the media on police and criminal matters and the respectable face for a number of television advertisements. After-dinner speaking, corporate presentations, product promotions, seminars, conferences and motivational talks became further vehicles for his talents as he built a new life for himself away from the police force which had almost destroyed him.

LOUISE WOODWARD: AMERICAN BABY MURDER CASE

For almost two years the small, quiet Cheshire village of Elton, near Chester, was the centre of an international media feeding frenzy. Local girl Louise Woodward was convicted by an American court of the murder of baby Matthew Eappen during her duties as an au pair to the American family while she was living in America. The televised murder trial in 1997 was one of the most notorious in American legal history and was seen worldwide, arousing strong emotions both for the prosecution and for the defence.

After the emergency services were first alerted, baby Eappen was rushed to hospital in a critical condition. During this time a police sergeant claimed that Louise Woodward changed her story and told him that she had dropped the baby. Louise denied making such a comment and said that it was the police who had put the words into her mouth. The evidence appeared to indicate that the baby had at least been severely shaken and had as a result suffered irreversible brain damage. Certainly the Eappen family believed and claimed that the 18-year-old nanny had murdered their baby. Their allegation caused great shock and outrage not only to Woodward's local villagers but also to the people of Britain.

The trial was highly controversial and the verdict of second-degree murder with a penalty of life imprisonment created further outrage in the UK and

Louise Woodward from Elton who was convicted in America for the manslaughter of a baby in her care. *(Chronicle Photographic)*

revulsion in the village of Elton. The villagers, believing in her innocence, rallied to defend her. On appeal the murder conviction was reduced to manslaughter, but the defence wanted to remove all trace of guilt while the prosecution wanted to reinstate the murder verdict and pushed for a jail term of at least fifteen years.

The Supreme Court of Massachusetts rejected the defence plea and upheld the conviction of manslaughter. The good news for Louise Woodward was the ruling by the judge who deemed that as she had already served 279 days in prison, that was sufficient punishment and she could be released and returned to the UK. The judge also ruled that neither Louise nor her family could profit from her crime and that she must never be permitted to be in charge of children ever again.

NEIL HAMILTON: CASH FOR QUESTIONS CASE

In the 1990s Cheshire was involved in yet another media frenzy when Tatton MP Neil Hamilton became embroiled in what was to prove to be one of the great parliamentary scandals.

Born in Blackwood, Wales, Hamilton rose through the Conservative political ranks and then, after marrying Christine in 1982, moved to Nether Alderley, Cheshire, in 1983 when he became MP for Tatton, a very safe Tory stronghold. He looked all set for a glittering career, his ebullient style singling him out for a series of high-profile government appointments such as Chairman of the Treasury and Civil Service Select Committee, government whip and Corporate Affairs Minister at the Department of Trade and Industry and representing Britain at the G7 conference.

Neil Hamilton, the former MP for Tatton, who was at the centre of the parliamentary cash-for-questions scandal in the 1990s. (*Knutsford Guardian*)

But it was not to last. Hamilton's rising profile and growing influence attracted the attention of parties interested only in pursuing their own ends. In 1987 Neil and Christine Hamilton were invited to spend six nights with all expenses paid (and they were considerable) in the hugely luxurious Ritz Hotel in Paris owned by Mohamed Al Fayed. Suspicions had been aroused during this time that some Members of Parliament were receiving cash or benefits in return for doing parliamentary favours for businessmen. However, it was not until October 1994 that the *Guardian* newspaper made allegations that Tim Smith and Neil Hamilton were two MPs who were accepting cash for raising questions in the House of Commons. Smith admitted it and resigned from the Tory Party; Hamilton denied it and issued a writ for libel against the *Guardian*, which he then dropped in September 1996. The *Guardian*, far from being grateful, made a statement on 1 October describing Hamilton as a cheat and a liar. Parliament was stung into action and an inquiry team was established in 1997 under watchdog Sir Gordon Downey to gather evidence from other MPs and also from the *Guardian* itself. On 16 January things really came to a head when in the Channel 4 television programme *Dispatches*, Mohamed Al Fayed openly admitted that he had paid Neil Hamilton several thousands of pounds delivered in brown envelopes, given him Harrods vouchers, and lavish hospitality at the Ritz in Paris, in return for Hamilton posing questions in Parliament on behalf of Al-Fayed's interests.

As the scandal raged there was severe pressure on Neil Hamilton to stand down from the 1997 general election. Journalist Martin Bell agreed to stand against Hamilton as an Independent on an anti-sleaze agenda, when Hamilton survived a constituency vote and confirmed that he would stand in the election. Bell won Tatton in May 1997 and Hamilton's parliamentary career was virtually over.

When it appeared that things could not get any worse, they did. In July Sir Gordon Downey's inquiry condemned Hamilton's behaviour. Now cast into the wilderness Hamilton decided to take action against Al-Fayed and on 16 January 1998 he took out a writ against him, so triggering off one of the biggest parliamentary trials in this country's history. The trial which would last for five weeks commenced on 15 November 1999 and dominated the newspapers, television and radio as allegation after allegation was countered by further allegation. Of Mohamed Al Fayed the judge advised the jury that, 'It would be very dangerous to accept even those parts of his evidence that you find credible and indeed you would be unwise to do so unless you are satisfied on evidence which you find highly convincing and find confirms Mr Fayed's evidence in a material way.' The judge also reminded the jury that Hamilton was accused of corruption not greed and suggested that Hamilton had been less than candid.

On 21 December 1999 the trial which had gripped the nation, ended. The jury found for Al-Fayed and agreed that on the balance of probabilities

Al-Fayed had established corruption by Hamilton on highly convincing evidence. The almost five-year battle by Hamilton to clear his name had ended in ruinous and inglorious defeat.

The *Guardian* felt vindicated by its decision to raise the issue in the first instance and demanded that Hamilton apologise to its reporters, whom he had maligned in trying to discredit their findings.

The Hamiltons, although facing financial ruin from the huge costs, vowed to take the fight to the European Court. An appeal to overturn the guilty verdict was lost and over the ensuing years the Hamiltons embarked on a whole series of ventures, media appearances, books, speeches and game shows in a determined effort to pay off their debts. In 2003 they eventually sold their Alderley Edge home, so severing their happy and sometimes painful connection with Cheshire. Their efforts did earn them considerable support from the public and helped to repair some of the damage to their image.

The Hamiltons certainly brought colour to Cheshire during their stay in the county. Were they infamous or were they the victims of infamy? They still believe that they are the victims.

PAUL BURRELL

A police raid on a house in the picturesque Cheshire village of Farndon precipitated one of the most controversial and sensational trials involving the royal family ever held in a British court.

Royal butler Paul Burrell, a resident of Farndon, was born in Derbyshire and after obtaining a diploma at the Hotel and Catering College in Buxton he joined the staff at Buckingham Palace as an 18-year-old footman in 1976. It was during a visit to Balmoral that he first met the young Lady Diana Spencer. She was a guest at the house and Burrell helped her to her room where they sat and talked for some time. Little did they know then that this was just the forerunner of many such sessions in the years to come.

In 1984 Burrell married Maria Cosgrove who was the Duke of Edinburgh's maid and the couple moved to Highgrove to work with the Prince and Princess of Wales. Soon the Burrells' children and Prince William and Prince Harry became friends, and when the royal marriage disintegrated and the couple parted, at Diana's request Paul moved with her to Kensington Palace as her personal butler.

As her marriage fell apart Diana had to cope not only with two children, but also with having to find a role in life and to deal with the hostility from those who felt that she had become too popular with the public and did not always behave appropriately. She was by all accounts acutely unhappy at times and she claimed Paul Burrell was her 'rock': a confidant, a shoulder to cry on and although he was always respectful, it was clear that his duties went far beyond that of personal servant as his book would later reveal.

After Diana's death in the Paris car crash, Burrell was entrusted with dressing her body for burial and getting rid of the bloodstained garment in which she had been killed. Quite clearly he enjoyed a high level of trust. However, with the death of Diana his world collapsed and at times he was close to breakdown. Wallowing in despair, he was nevertheless selected to head the fund-raising campaign for the Diana, Princess of Wales Memorial Fund. It was a position he revelled in. Organising and fronting dinner functions, invitations to galas and Hollywood fundraisers, he enjoyed the high life and the spotlight. After only a short time in the job he was made redundant. It was hinted that some people had become disillusioned with him.

Undeterred, he continued to make a living on the back of his royal connections: engaging in after-dinner speaking, writing newspaper columns on etiquette, lecturing on cruise liners and also publishing a book about royal food and dining. But his cosy world was about to change drastically.

On a winter's night in January 2001, acting on a tip-off, the police raided Paul Burrell's home in Farndon, Cheshire. They searched the house, including the attic, looking for items belonging to the Princess's estate and took away many items. In June 2001 Burrell was charged with stealing more than 300 items from the estate of the Princess of Wales. During the investigations the police had informed Prince Charles, Prince William and Prince Harry that they had evidence of Paul Burrell selling items belonging to the late Princess.

The case came to trial in November 2002 with Burrell insisting that he was innocent of any wrongdoing and repeating that he had never sold any of Diana's possessions. Furthermore he said that he had conclusive proof of his innocence and stated that he had only been acting as custodian of Diana's possessions (photographs, letters, dresses, documents, etc.) to protect them for the royal family. He stated that he had informed the Queen and other members of the royal family after Diana's death and had received their approval for his actions. Despite his statement and with no acknowledgement coming from the royal family, the trial continued to dominate the headlines.

Then, sensationally, in a move unparalleled in British history, the Queen intervened in the trial and confirmed that Paul Burrell had indeed told her that he was in possession of a number of Diana's belongings and was retaining them for safe keeping. The trial, which had cost £1.5 million, collapsed and Paul Burrell walked from the court fully acquitted of all charges.

Many issues were raised following this sensational case. Who had tipped the police off in the first instance? Why had the police lied when telling Prince Charles that they had evidence of Burrell selling Diana's belongings, when they had no such evidence? Why didn't Prince Charles intervene earlier? Indeed why did the Queen 'remember' the Burrell conversation so late in the trial?

Back in his home village of Farndon the locals were ecstatic following Burrell's victory. He was very popular in the small village and owned a florist's shop, Paul Burrell's Flowers and Gifts, in the nearby tiny village of Holt, a few hundred yards away over the border into Wrexham where his wife Maria had grown up. Nationally there was a great deal of sympathy for him, with the vast majority of the public believing that his devotion to Diana had evoked vindictive responses from those less sympathetic to her cause. There was also a feeling that the same powers that had persecuted Diana had contrived to persecute her faithful servant Paul Burrell.

However, the wave of public sympathy was somewhat diluted when in October 2003 Paul Burrell's book, *A Royal Duty*, hit the shops. It revealed stories of life below stairs, the duties of the 300 or so staff at the palace, the petty jealousies and squabbles and the inside stories on sex, drinking and

Paul Burrell, the former royal butler, outside his flower shop in the village of Holt. *(Chronicle Photographic/Haydn Ball)*

gambling. He covered the ten years he gave personal service to the Queen, his work with Prince Charles and then the Diana years.

Some of the revelations were regarded by many to be at best in bad taste, and they caused great hurt and embarrassment to the young princes who went so far as to request him to stop revealing details which would tarnish their mother's memory. It was clear that they felt he had not only betrayed Diana but also themselves, who at one point in their lives had got to know and to trust him. Burrell held a press conference at Rowton Hall, Cheshire, during which he said he was saddened by the princes' statement. He defended his book saying that he was extremely proud of it, as it was a tribute to their mother and urged the princes to read it, as he felt that they would then have a different opinion.

Great swathes of the media and the public took exception to many of the revelations and Burrell lost a lot of support and goodwill. Many believed that he had cashed in on Diana's memory, having always stated that this loyalty and devotion to her would never be up for sale. The *Daily Mirror*, for example, paid him £300,000 for his story following his trial acquittal and then paid him an undisclosed sum to publish extracts from his book.

Burrell decided, according to the newspapers in January 2004, to leave Britain in the summer to settle with his wife and two sons in a house he had purchased in Florida. In 2004 he launched a series of travelling talk shows, *Paul Burrell In His Own Words*, dedicated to fans of the Princess of Wales both in the UK and on Broadway. However, three of the four shows were cancelled on Broadway owing to poor ticket sales. Burrell's appearance in 2004 in the reality television programme, *I'm A Celebrity, Get Me Out Of Here* did something to redeem him. The public are asked to judge how the contestants are coping in a tropical jungle, stripped of luxuries and scrutinised by the intimate and intrusive fly-on-the-wall cameras. Each week one of the celebrities is judged to be a failure and voted off the programme. During one of a number of tasks, a terrified and disgusted Burrell had to eat live insects. He completed the challenge and proved that he had the mental strength to cope with adversity. His performances earned him the respect of the viewing public and he finished the programme as runner-up to the eventual winner.

At one low point in his life Paul Burrell may have had every reason to believe that the 'grey suits' were quite prepared to see him go to prison before relenting at the last moment. Did he betray Diana's memory? Hero or villain? Victim of infamy or perpetrator?

CHRIS EVANS: GAMBLED AND LOST £15 MILLION

Cheshire's knack of being involved in spectacular High Court actions continued with a particularly high-profile show-business action involving

Chris Evans, who was born in Warrington in 1966. The case concluded with one of the most damning, cutting personal statements ever delivered by a High Court judge. Not only did the case cost Evans an estimated £15 million when the judgment went against him, but Mr Justice Lightman devastatingly described him as a 'petulant, bingeing liar'.

In what must be seen as one of the most spectacular own goals ever scored, Evans was suing his former employers Virgin Radio for wrongful dismissal. Virgin Radio had offered him a payment of £3 million if he would settle out of court but Evans decided to sue.

Although disliked by many he nevertheless has a talent and an eye for business. Ginger-haired and overconfident, with thick black-rimmed glasses, his individual style as a broadcaster, first in Manchester with Radio Piccadilly

Chris Evans with a fan. *(Warrington Guardian)*

and then with Greater London Radio, earned him early recognition. It was *The Big Breakfast* television show in 1992 which gave him the big break. Television and radio performing came to him easily and soon he formed Ginger Productions and started producing his own programmes. The television show *Don't Forget Your Toothbrush* was a huge success and was eventually sold to more than twenty countries.

Evans was lured back to radio in a £500,000 deal to present the *Breakfast Show* on Radio 1. It was hugely successful, featuring outrageous comment, laddish stunts and occasional outbursts of arrogance from Evans to his own staff, live on air. A television opportunity with Channel 4 to front *TFI Friday* brought even greater success and became cult viewing, with many stars and celebrities trying to get on the show. In the meantime Chris Evans was still presenting for Radio 1 and asked his boss for permission to have Fridays off to give him more time to prepare for the television show. His request was refused and Evans walked out on Radio 1 in 1997.

When *TFI Friday* eventually started to lose its appeal Channel 4 dropped the show, which left Evans still presenting a breakfast show with Virgin Radio. Evans shrewdly bought the radio station from Richard Branson for £80 million and followed that by selling Ginger Productions, which also owned Virgin Radio, to the Scottish Media Group for £225 million. An astute piece of business dealing, it is believed that he made close to £75 million profit on the transaction. Although it appeared that he frequently acted like an idiot, in terms of business he was far from it. Evans was then employed as a presenter by Virgin Radio.

The spectacular fall from grace via the High Court ruling was prompted when Evans wanted to present an all-day programme prior to the England World Cup soccer-qualifying match against Greece in 2001. When his bosses said 'no', Evans once again walked out and then, it is said, indulged in a drinking bout which lasted for three days. He did not appear for work, but did appear at his local pub, with his wife Billie Piper, for the entire world to see. It was seen as a deliberate act of defiance by a spoilt child who had been told 'no'. Virgin sacked him and Evans then threatened to sue, stating that he had been unable to work due to illness.

When giving his verdict after the court case in June 2003, Mr Justice Lightman was clearly unimpressed with Evans and delivered a devastating summary. Ruling in favour of Virgin Radio he said, 'Evans was unprofessional, manipulative, insecure, sulking and childish. He was the kind of man who would resort to any means "fair or foul" to get his way.' Furthermore, he added, 'He was a person who could not tolerate personal criticism or management authority. He was holding two fingers up, inviting Virgin to take action if it dared.'

Despite the unfavourable outcome, Evans has bounced back with a new contract for Radio 2.

THE INFAMOUS EGG 'POACHER'

Cheshire (Runcorn, to be precise) is the home of Britain's most notorious and infamous egg collector. In what was heralded as a major triumph, the Royal Society for the Protection of Birds was delighted when Anthony Higham pleaded guilty to thirteen charges under the Wildlife and Countryside Act 1981 and the Control of Trade and Endangered Species Regulations of 1997 at his trial on 10 April 2003.

It was due to the action of Merseyside police in March 2002 when they arrested Carlton D'Cruze, another egg collector, which led to the successful investigation of Higham. When Cheshire police raided his home in Runcorn they found documentation, containers and outdoor equipment which indicated that he was involved in egg collecting. He was arrested and charged with possession but refused to help the police while protesting his innocence. Further investigations, again by Merseyside police, resulted in a second search warrant in Widnes, which led to the finding of Higham's hidden 'treasure'. The police find not only staggered and dismayed the RSPB, but wildlife enthusiasts everywhere.

More than 800 eggs were found, including those of golden eagles, divers, choughs, peregrines and ospreys, all Schedule One protected species. Further evidence, journals, photographs and a damning video of Higham and D'Cruze actively taking eggs in the countryside made another arrest inevitable and guilt overwhelming. When faced with the evidence Higham admitted his involvement and indeed led authorities to a find of eight more clutches of eggs.

At his trial the magistrate ruled that the offences had been deliberate, were planned and persistent (he had been involved for more than ten years) and were therefore very serious.

On 10 April Higham was sentenced at Northwich Magistrates Court to four months in prison. The option to impose a prison sentence for breaching the Wildlife Act was introduced in 2001 and Anthony Higham became only the sixth egg 'poacher' to be jailed, but he was Britain's most prolific egg stealer.

Why he, or indeed anyone, should want to steal the eggs, the lifeblood of magnificent endangered species whose existence they purport to cherish is bizarre.

TERRY WAITE: IMPRISONED WITHOUT TRIAL

Cheshire-born Terry Waite was imprisoned in the Lebanon for almost five years without trial.

Born in Bollington in 1939 and raised in Styal, the young Terence moved with his family to Thelwall. He joined the Church and gradually progressed through the ranks, gaining experience in Africa before becoming a consultant to the Roman Catholic Church from 1972 to 1979. His ordeal followed his appointment as Advisor to the Archbishop of Canterbury, Robert Runcie, in 1980. Much valued by Runcie, Waite was sent out to Beirut in 1987 to utilise his diplomatic skills to negotiate the release of European hostages taken by Islamic fundamentalists. Despite all the warnings about the risk he was taking and the dangers he faced, Waite did not flinch from his task. The fundamentalists did not share his ethics and against all protocol they captured Waite, imprisoned him and subjected him to severe deprivation.

Waite's ordeal is well documented in his book *Taken On Trust* published after his release in 1991. For most of his imprisonment Waite was held in isolation, chained to radiators, moved from house to house usually tied and blindfolded in the boot of a car, beaten with electric cables, starved and frequently subjected to brainwashing. At times he was close to despair and madness, but his faith carried him through.

He wrote several books in the years following his release and was soon leading an active life. In February 2004 Waite visited his old haunts, in particular Beirut, as part of his mission investigating the conditions in the Palestinian refugee camp in North Beirut. While walking in the streets a man approached him and asked Waite if he remembered him? Waite gazed only for an instant at the small, chubby figure wearing a bobble hat before embracing the man in a bear hug. He exclaimed in front of the journalists with him, 'Hussein, of course I remember you.' Hussein had been Waite's trusted driver and had been with him when he was kidnapped and had raised the alarm.

Terry Waite survived because of his strong will and his faith, but he was undoubtedly the victim of a terrible act of infamy.

7

CALLOUS
BEYOND BELIEF

Since the dawn of civilisation murder has been the ultimate crime: man's final solution to the frustrations and inadequacies created by greed, fear, jealousy or passion. Despite greater education, more awareness of human rights, deterrents and punishments, murder as a final solution will regrettably haunt man until the end of time.

Cheshire's towns have witnessed their share of murders: Stockport, Crewe, Congleton, Hyde, Birkenhead, Bramhall, Dukinfield, Stalybridge, New Brighton, Altrincham, Alderley Edge, Warrington, Knutsford, Northwich, Winsford, Liscard, Mouldsworth, Widnes, Ellesmere Port, Neston and Smallwood, to name but a few, not forgetting Macclesfield, which has witnessed several.

Although murder can never be condoned, there are instances when it is perhaps understandable. Where, for example, human frailty has snapped or given way to basic instincts driven by fear, the need for revenge or an attempt to protect loved ones. Indeed murder can arise as the result of an action which was not intended. However, there are instances where murder so brutal, so heinous, so sadistic, so horrific and so pre-meditated defies all understanding.

Regrettably, Cheshire has witnessed several such cases in recent times, including Britain's most prolific serial killer and arguably the nation's most infamous killer, 'Jack the Ripper'.

CONGLETON CANNIBAL

One particularly brutal and heinous murder occurred in November 1776 and created the legend of the 'Congleton Cannibal'. From the evidence of the time it would seem that the perpetrator, Sam Thorley, was something of a simpleton and perhaps today would be regarded as unfit to plead and confined to hospital care.

On a cold November morning farmer Newman Garside, with a helper, was herding his cows into a field in nearby Astbury when his attention was caught by a blue cloak floating in the small brook running through the field. Their investigations also revealed a bloodstained yellow gown. Alarmed, they shouted to two men working in a nearby field to come and help them. A thorough search of the surrounding area uncovered a dastardly deed. Scattered alongside a petticoat, a black ribbon, a lady's small bag containing a half-eaten brown loaf, and a small cap, were a woman's arm and a leg, half a right arm and another leg severed at the knee. Worse was to come as severed breasts, bowels, tongue and other body parts were found scattered in the grass. The eventual location of the head identified the body as that of Ann Smith, a 22-year-old local girl. The police were called and very soon Sam Thorley was arrested after a local man, Thomas Cordwell, overheard him talking about the murder.

At the time Thorley was certainly a prime suspect. A big man, he was known to be difficult and moody with a sharp temper. He did odd jobs around the area digging graves at Astbury church and he often worked for the local butcher hacking and dissecting animal carcasses and was known to eat raw animal meat. Cordwell, with all the instincts of a modern-day sleuth, searched local barns for signs of bloodstains, then visited the cottage where Thorley had lodged with a local woman, Hanah Oakes. She confirmed that Thorley had lodged there for a few days and the other night had returned with an apron full of meat saying that it was pork from a pig he had killed earlier that day. Dropping the clump of meat on the table he had asked Hanah to boil it for him. However, she hadn't liked the look of it and had refused. Thorley, she said, had then placed the meat in cold storage and the next night, having boiled and eaten some of it, had been violently sick. Thorley had gone to Astbury to collect his wages so Cordwell asked if she would show him the rest of the meat. Cordwell was convinced that it was human and the local surgeon later confirmed his fears.

The police searched for Thorley and after arresting him locked him in the Congleton Town Hall before sending him to Chester Assizes for trial, charged with the murder of Ann Smith. Although fully detailed records of the trial do not exist, it was said that Thorley had no defence, seemed unperturbed and showed no remorse. He was said to have admitted that he thought human flesh tasted like pork and he wanted to try some.

No reason for the killing was ever established but conjecture had it that the couple had met while walking through the fields and she had borrowed his knife to cut her bread and cheese and perhaps had teased him, as he was regarded as a simpleton. Maybe he had tried to force himself upon her in return for his favour. Whatever it was, it goaded him into cutting her throat and then butchering her.

Thorley was found guilty and was hanged at Boughton on 10 April 1777 before being gibbeted and his body suspended at West Heath, close to where he had committed the murder, as a warning to others. Ann Smith was buried at Astbury church on 24 November 1776.

JACK THE RIPPER: SEVERIN KLOSOWSKI ALIAS GEORGE CHAPMAN

One of the most fascinating and intriguing mysteries of Victorian England is the enduring legend of Jack the Ripper, so named for his series of particularly gruesome murders in the gas-lit Whitechapel area of London. Although not as prolific a killer (he had five victims) as many modern-day serial killers, the nature of his actions horrified the nation between his first killing on 31 August 1888, and his last killing in November 1888. The 'Ripper' targeted prostitutes, disembowelling his victims, cutting throats and removing sexual organs and on occasion dissecting the bodies. London was, for a time, gripped with fear, not knowing where or when the killer would strike next, and then the murders mysteriously ceased, but the killer was never found.

To this day there is still speculation as to his identity, with theories ranging from a deranged psychopathic surgeon to a member of the royal family which would explain why his identity was never revealed.

However, a man with Cheshire connections has been proposed as Jack the Ripper by at least two highly respected police officers familiar with the case: Detective Inspector Frederick Abbeline and Detective Superintendent Arthur Fowler Neil, who in his book *40 Years of Manhunting*, stated that George Chapman, formerly Severin Klosowski, was a very likely candidate.

Klosowski was born in Poland in 1865 and for a time worked as an apprentice to a surgeon performing minor operations. He completed his course at a Warsaw hospital where records reveal that he was an enthusiastic student of surgery. He married in Poland and in the early 1880s came to England but there is no record of why he left Poland and his wife. Early accounts say that he worked as a pub assistant and then as a barber's assistant. During this period he worked and lived in Whitechapel High Street, the area at the centre of the Ripper's activities. In October 1889 he married Lucy Baderski, a Polish girl. A son was born in 1890, but after his tragic death in 1891 the couple moved to Jersey City, New Jersey, America and established a barber's shop in their house, but in 1892 they split up and the pregnant Lucy returned alone to the UK. Later that year Klosowski also returned to the UK and for a short time they were reconciled.

This gap would explain the end of the Ripper's series of murders. He had met someone, fallen in love and moved to America, the ideal scenario for an end to his murderous activities. Only it wasn't the end, but perhaps merely a change in *modus operandi*.

Within months of leaving Lucy he moved in with Annie Chapman and, despite her becoming pregnant, the relationship ended in 1894 after a series of arguments over his womanising. It was during this period that he changed his name to George Chapman.

He met Mary Isabella Spink and after allegedly marrying her, they started a hairdressing business and after a great deal of success moved into the pub

Bessie and George Chapman. Is this the face of Jack the Ripper? *(Courtesy of Alan Hayhurst)*

trade, taking over the Prince of Wales tavern. Despite their success and relative prosperity it was known at this time that Chapman frequently beat his wife. What wasn't known was that he had also started treating her with small doses of poison. On Christmas Day 1897 Mary Spink died after suffering for several days with severe stomach pains. The cause of death was given as tuberculosis.

Victim number two arrived in the buxom form of Cheshire farmer's daughter Elizabeth (Bessie) Taylor who appeared in response to a newspaper advertisement announcing a vacancy at the pub at Easter 1898. Bessie had been born and raised on a farm at Booths Hill in Lymm, and had made the move to London in her early 20s. At the time of meeting Chapman she had been in the London area for ten years and had good experience in the food and drink industry.

By all accounts she was fit and well and it is believed that as she got to know Chapman better she took him to Lymm to meet her family. Chapman came to the village several times and stayed in the same local inn. He was sociable; indeed at one time he entered a smoking concert (for men only) and treated the locals to champagne. Again, although no official records can confirm the fact, it is said that the couple later married. Towards the end of 1898 Bessie went into hospital with a nasty illness and after she had recovered in early 1899, it was apparent that Chapman's feelings for her had changed. The relationship deteriorated, as did Bessie's health. Friends and

Was Bessie Chapman a victim of Jack the Ripper? Her surname was removed by the Taylors from the family headstone. *(Lymm Local History Society/ Joe Griffiths/John King)*

The Taylor family headstone marking the burial place of Bessie. *(Lymm Local History Society/Joe Griffiths/John King)* family were shocked by her frailty and weakness. On 13 February 1901 she died, aged 36. Various causes of death were given by several doctors: severe constipation, cancer of the stomach, infected womb and intestinal obstruction. None of them suspected poisoning. Chapman's last visit to the Cheshire village was to Bessie's funeral.

Events leading to the death on 22 October 1901 of his third victim, barmaid Maud Marsh, followed a similar pattern: new barmaid falls under Chapman's spell, he 'marries her', she falls ill and dies. On this occasion doctors realised too late that Marsh had been deliberately killed. The other victims were exhumed and it was found that they had all been poisoned by antimony. Chapman was arrested.

As the Chapman case hit the headlines, similarities between him and the Ripper began to emerge. A woman with whom he had lived in London at the time of the Ripper terror in the Whitechapel area, recalled that Chapman often disappeared into the night and would return at about three or four o'clock in the morning without any explanation.

A friend of one of the Ripper's victims gave a good description of a man seen talking to her at about two o'clock in the morning. He was 34 or 35, 5ft 6in tall, surly with a pale face, dark eyes, dark hair and a small moustache that curled up at both ends. His dress consisted of a long dark coat with a collar and cuffs trimmed in astrakhan, buttoned boots with gaiters and white buttons. Distinctively, he was said to wear a very thick gold chain and a horseshoe pin. In short, a bit of a snappy dresser, a dandy.

In November 1902 the local paper, the *Warrington Guardian*, when commenting on Chapman's murder of local girl Bessie Taylor, confirmed the impression of him being a snappy dresser when describing him as a 'toff', dressed stylishly with many rings and a heavy gold chain. The physical similarities were also marked, apart from the age difference. At the time of the Ripper killings Chapman was about 23. At the time of *The Warrington Guardian* report the newspaper had no idea of a possible link between Chapman and the Ripper.

George Chapman was tried and, despite his protestations of innocence, found guilty of murder and hanged at Wandsworth Gaol on Tuesday 7 April 1903.

It is unlikely after all these years that the true identity of Jack the Ripper will ever be known. Although Detective Inspector Frederick Abbeline and Detective Superintendent Arthur Fowler Neil believe that Chapman was a real suspect, other experts doubt it. One of the major reasons for their doubts is the break of nine years and then a completely different series of killings.

Chapman did fall in love and move to America so had a golden opportunity to mend his ways. The failure of his marriage and the eventual return to his old haunts may well have triggered off his suppressed hatred for women. His business and married status gave him the ideal respectable cover to indulge in a new and less bloody way of satisfying his evil impulses. Certainly he fitted the description, he lived in the area, he had a limited experience of surgical work, he was known to frequent the night and he enjoyed murdering women.

Doubters at first said that there was no evidence of Chapman using knives in the murders of his 'wives' and found it difficult to accept the argument that he as the Ripper had merely changed his *modus operandi*. Chapman's real wife, Lucy Klosowski, attended the trials and it was reported in the *Daily Chronicle* on 23 March 1903 that she had told the newspaper of an incident during their marriage when perhaps, for a moment, she had glimpsed Jack the Ripper and lived to tell the tale.

She recounted that on one occasion when running their hairdresser business in New Jersey they had started to argue. As the row became more heated Klosowski (he hadn't changed his name at that time) threw her onto the bed and pressed his face very firmly across her mouth to stop her screaming. Just at that point the bell rang and a customer came into the shop that was literally in the next room. Klosowski was forced to release her and went to attend to the client. Relieved, she sat up and, as her senses returned, she saw a handle protruding from beneath a pillow. Lifting the pillow she was horrified to find a large, sharp knife. She hid it. Later she asked him what the knife was for. He chillingly told her that he had intended to cut off her head then bury her in a corner of the room. When she countered that the neighbours would have missed her and would have asked where she was, he said that he was going to tell them that she had gone to New York.

Unsurprisingly the marriage did not survive for long after that incident and she returned to England. Their subsequent brief reconciliation seems surprising but was perhaps for the sake of their child. As it turned out, Lucy was a very fortunate lady: she escaped a possible butchering and a probable poisoning.

The Taylor family removed the name of Chapman from their family headstone in the small graveyard at the parish church, Lymm. For quite some time following the trial and the subsequent hanging of Chapman, the curious turned up in great numbers, sometimes coachloads, to view the headstone at the tiny church. In a final bizarre touch, George Chapman left a sum of £140 to the relatives of the murdered Bessie Taylor in his last will and testament. Perhaps he had a soft spot for Cheshire, remembering the walks along the country lanes and drinking in the village pubs of Lymm.

There is strong evidence that Chapman was Jack the Ripper. Cheshire may well have played host to history's most infamous murderer.

MOULDSWORTH MURDERS

Claudine Liebert and her fiancé, Daniel Bernard, both 20, and her sister Monique Liebert aged 22, were enjoying a leisurely holiday in Britain in

July 1971 touring around in their Citroën car, camping where their fancy took them with all the freedom so relished by young people on the threshold of life.

On the gloriously sunny Sunday of 11 July, the three youngsters arrived near the village of Mouldsworth and called in at the Goshawk pub for a drink and to decide their destination for the night. Too tired to go much further and liking the area anyway, they decided to pitch camp in the vicinity and round about 10.30 p.m. found a little clearing in Woodside close to Mouldsworth and the Delamere Forest.

As fate would have it someone else was also heading towards Delamere Forest, it is believed ostensibly to commit suicide. Michael Bassett, aged 24, could be classed as one of life's losers. For one so young he had certainly tried his hand at a variety of career options: as a book salesman, a writer, a musician and odd-job man. Life had become an unequal struggle and it is believed that the rejection of his latest novel by a publisher had sent him over the edge. He had decided to take a short break in Rhyl where, as his depression deepened, he broke into a fairground stall and stole a .22 rifle. Hell-bent on a final solution, Bassett drove away from Rhyl destined for the Delamere Forest and oblivion.

The following day, Monday 12 July, a man on his way to work at 7 a.m. saw the young people's tent and then, to his horror, saw sprawled outside the tent the naked, lifeless, bloodstained body of Claudine. Inside the tent, Daniel was also dead but Monique was still clinging to life. Despite being rushed to hospital and receiving an emergency operation, she died of her wounds.

Police discovered that more than twenty shots had been fired in what clearly was a callous, cold-blooded, merciless massacre of the defenceless youngsters. There were no witnesses but neighbours did report hearing the sound of a car leaving the vicinity at about 2 a.m., but that was all.

The identity of the killer was quickly revealed when on 13 July the police in Stone, Staffordshire, came across a parked car containing a dead body. Suicide through exhaust fumes and a final scrawled note, 'They provoked me. I taught them a lesson', left little room for doubt that this was the perpetrator of the Mouldsworth killings. There was a further message from Bassett scratched out on the butt of the rifle which police found tucked under an arm. 'It killed three campers.' Another note seemed to indicate the twisted state of his mind when it noted that by the time it was found he would be in a happier place. It would seem that Bassett had tired of life and failure and, whatever had happened that horrendous night, there had been no sexual motive, no robbery.

Why and how had he come across the youngsters, who presumably had settled down for the night, when he was presumed to have been looking for solitude and a quiet place to end it all? Perhaps with a final nasty twist he simply decided to end the lives of others whom he perceived to be enjoying life.

PRESTBURY BANK MURDERS

Callous and cold-blooded as the Mouldsworth murders undoubtedly were, they certainly rank below the Prestbury bank murders of 1977 in terms of premeditated calculating and cruel acts.

Prestbury, about a mile from Macclesfield, is renowned in Cheshire and indeed in Britain for being one of the wealthiest villages in the country. It has magnificent houses in the several-million-pound bracket, an exclusive golf club, a quaint old church, superb restaurants and a High Street right out of a Dickens novel. Black and white timbered buildings, quality but quaint shops and plush cars line the village streets. Behind this façade of wealth and good taste there is a modest little black and white building which today houses a branch of the Royal Bank of Scotland, but also keeps a dark secret.

The village of Prestbury, scene of the Prestbury bank murders in 1977. *(Bob Burrows)*

The former Williams and Glyn's Bank building, Prestbury, where one person was murdered and another abducted in 1977. *(Bob Burrows)*

Back in February 1977 the building contained a small branch of the Williams and Glyn's Bank, and was the site of a murderous crime so horrific that it sickened the whole country. The branch was manned normally by two staff who travelled the short distance from the main branch in Macclesfield each day to give a service to the village. Being such a small branch in such a friendly, affluent village it was usually a pleasure to be asked to work there as the customers appreciated a warm, personal service.

On 25 February 1977 the branch was anything but a friendly place to work. Indeed it quickly became a house of horrors. Ian Jebb, aged 21, a young man who was engaged to be married, had been appointed under-manager to give him further experience and, together with 19-year-old Susan Hockenull, travelled from Macclesfield to staff the branch on what should have been a routine day. Susan, a local girl from Gawsworth, enjoyed working on the bank counter and being involved with the customers.

The addition to the equation on that fateful day was the visit to the branch of service engineer David Walsh from Macclesfield who had called at the branch to carry out a service operation on the adding machine. Unbeknown to the two youngsters, Walsh was in financial difficulties and was planning to steal cash from the bank. It was later revealed that he had received a distress warrant for rent arrears on his council house, had outstanding debts on his car and on a motorbike. He knew that his best opportunity would come when the branch closed from 12.30 to 1.30 p.m. to enable the staff to have a lunch break.

The branch closed as normal and later during the break Susan was seen walking with a man in the main street. It was remembered by the witness that they were walking very closely together and he was carrying a briefcase.

At 1.30 p.m. the branch didn't open and a queue had started to form. There was no response to knocks on the door and eventually the local head office at Macclesfield was notified and they immediately sent staff out to investigate.

The branch soon gave up its secret. The bound and gagged body of Ian Jebb was found on the floor in a pool of blood. It later transpired that he had been struck on the head and then stabbed in the back twice and in the heart twice. Of Susan, who must have witnessed this terrifying slaying, there was no sign.

The next day the body of Susan Hockenhull was found purely by chance in an isolated spot in the hills on New Zealand Farm, Meerbrook, Staffordshire. Walsh had frogmarched her through the village and then driven her almost 13 miles to a desolate location, tied her hands and feet, gagged her and then placed her, wearing only her indoor clothes, in a field in the depths of a English winter in sub-zero temperatures. Unable to move or to make a sound the terrified youngster froze to death.

Walsh was quickly identified as the prime suspect and police searches found new bank notes and coins under floorboards in his house. Despite all the evidence against him, Walsh protested his innocence, 'I'm a crook, but not a murderer.' He was tried on 10 October 1977 and was unanimously found guilty of murder and sentenced to a minimum of twenty-five years in prison.

It would be difficult to find a more cruel, premeditated crime than this. As soon as the bank door closed for lunch Walsh had attacked Jebb and when he was helpless had stabbed him unmercifully to death, perhaps even in front of young Susan. From that moment, she too was condemned and he knew when he took her away that he was going to kill her. She had to be silenced.

As the good people of Prestbury go about their business, how many glance at that small white building, proudly displaying the Royal Bank of Scotland sign, and remember or even know of the terrible struggle for life on that cold February day back in 1977?

BRITAIN'S WORST SERIAL KILLER

The small Cheshire town of Hyde (now in Greater Manchester) with its many back streets of terraced housing, smart semi-detached dwellings and homes for the elderly was the unlikeliest of killing fields for Britain's most notorious murderer.

Small, bearded, bespectacled, grey haired, respected and trusted he prowled the streets of this small town for more than twenty years murdering, on a massive scale, as the whim took him. Confident to the point of arrogance – after all he had the most perfect of all disguises – he was the most revered family doctor to more than 3,000 patients. He sated himself without public fear or anxiety because nobody knew that there was a problem.

Harold Shipman, the family doctor turned serial killer. *(Greg Smith/ Thameside Reporter)*

Dr Harold Shipman was eventually arrested in September 1998 and later convicted of murdering fifteen of his patients by administering to them a lethal injection of diamorphine. However, it is believed that he killed at least 215 people and some experts put the figure as high as 264.

Shipman was born in Nottingham on 14 June 1946 and at the age of 17 watched his 43-year-old mother die a slow death from cancer despite the efforts of the doctors to save her. Some psychologists believe that this tragic event may well have shaped Shipman's life and his mental state.

He studied medicine and at the age of 20 he married his pregnant 17-year-old girlfriend, Primrose. He qualified at university and in 1974 he became a GP in Todmorden. It is here as a 28-year-old young doctor that he committed his first murder, undetected.

In late 1975 it was discovered by his colleagues that he had been prescribing large doses of the drug pethedrine for himself and was forced to resign. His career should have ended here and many lives would have been saved. However, revealing a cunning which would stay with him all of his life, he stated that he was clearly ill and was in need of psychiatric treatment. Before entering the hospital he was found guilty by magistrates of seventy-five drug offences, forgery and possession and heavily fined. He now had a police record.

Shipman spent six months in the hospital and in less than a year he returned to medicine, working in a family planning centre in County Durham. The General Medical Council did not intervene. Several weeks later he was appointed a partner at the Donneybrook practice in Hyde. His reinstatement was complete, his disguise perfect. The killings could commence.

In 1993, after sixteen years working with the Donneybrook practice and building up a considerable reputation and following as a caring, hard-working GP, he decided to set up on his own and took over premises at 21 Market Street, Hyde, with a very strong immediate base of patients who appreciated his personal style. Now working on his own he could indulge himself without interference, without having to answer to anyone. His appetite quickened.

During his time at Donneybrook – almost sixteen years – he murdered seventy-one patients without any suspicion and remained undetected. No wonder that he felt untouchable, with the power to decide who should die and who should live. His reign at Market Street would last for almost six years, during which time he would murder about 190 people.

In the main his victims were elderly and female. Of the 215 known deaths only 44 were male. Not many families in Hyde escaped the carnage: whole streets had someone or knew someone who had been killed by Shipman. On occasion there were several victims from the same family. Unquestionably, Shipman had a hold over these patients and to a great extent over their families. His practice received numerous cards and sometimes flowers from relatives thanking him for his services and indeed after his arrest many, convinced of his innocence, sent cards and letters.

When people belatedly began to ask questions about the number of death certificates from the same practice early in 1998 the police, in response to local concerns, started to investigate. The first investigation was bungled and Shipman went on to commit three more murders before a rare mistake which gave him a motive for his last murder, that of Kathleen Grundy, finally pinned him down. He tried to forge Mrs Grundy's will to enable him to benefit by £360,000.

Following his arrest and subsequent trial Shipman never once admitted his guilt and indeed was often arrogant and dismissive of the police and their questions. Even after being found guilty and during the subsequent years in prison, he never gave any indication as to the motive for the killings. There

Harold Shipman's surgery in Hyde. *(Bob Burrows)*

was no obvious motive. In only one case did he refer to a patient as being a nuisance and in only one case was financial gain a possible reason. The real reason lies within the man. The murders often appeared to be random and although he killed five patients in the treatment room of his practice, the rest were carried out in the victims' own homes. The motive could not have been the joy of watching others suffer because the victims slipped away peacefully while Shipman, in many cases, sat in front of them.

Robbery was not really a motive although on one or two occasions he was known to have taken a piece of jewellery. Sexual satisfaction was not a motive as none of the victims had ever shown any signs of molestation. A top psychiatrist firmly believes that Shipman was a classic necrophiliac who derived satisfaction from the power of being able to cause death and to be in control of the victim's final moments.

Shipman resisted all attempts at a closure and on Tuesday 13 January 2004 he committed suicide by hanging himself in his cell at Wakefield maximum-security prison. His suicide created new waves of anguish and protests as the relatives realised that he had taken the coward's way out and real closure for them would now never happen.

Shipman is certainly Britain's worst serial killer, but not just numerically. The murders he committed were cold-blooded, calculating and cruel. Not only was he regarded as a kind, friendly doctor always willing to visit his patients, but also he was trusted by patients and their families. Even more cruel was the fact that he knew the victims' families and was aware of the suffering his actions would cause. After all, he was himself a family man with a daughter and three sons. He even murdered four relatives of one of his own receptionists. He also sent cards of condolence to the families of his victims. Callous in the extreme.

INDEX

A537 road 34–6
Abbeline, Det Insp
    Frederick 124, 127
Agnew, Jonathan 58, 59
Al Fayed, Mohamed 67,
    94
Anne, Queen 12, 13
Archbishop of Canterbury
    121
archers 1, 5
Ashes, The 39–43
Axon, John 43, 44

Badenski, Lucy 124
Barlow, Elizabeth 101, 102
Bell, Martin 67–70, 94
Benn, Nigel 94
Bennett, Steve 86, 87
Big Breakfast, The 119
Biggs, Ronnie 44, 45
Bishop of Chester 22, 81, 82
Bligh, Honourable Ivo 43
Boden, Mike 60
Boleyn, Anne 7
Bonnie, Prince Charles 17
Bradshaw, Lord Judge John
    14–16
Branson, Richard 119
Brereton, Sir William 7
Brocklehurst, Capt H.C. 78
Brocklehurst, Thomas Unett
    76, 78
Bromley Davenport, Lt Col
    Sir Walter 79, 80, 81
Bruche Police Training
    College 32–4
burned, at the stake, 22
Burrell, Paul 114–7

Capesthorne Hall 79, 80
Carey, Patrick 24

Catton, Dee 97, 98
Chapman, Annie 124
Chapman, George 124–8
Charles I 14, 15
Charles II 14
Charles, Prince 115, 117
Chelsea Football Club 84
Chinese cocklers 96
Clare, John 25, 27
Clowes, Peter 101–5
Congleton Cannibal 122,
    123
Congleton Museum 15, 26
Cromwell, Oliver 14–6
Cumberland, Duke of 17
Curtis, Ian 56

Daly, Mark 32, 33
Davidson, Paul 85–6
Diana, Princess of Wales
    114, 115, 117
Downey, Sir Gordon 67, 70
Doyle, Martin 27
Druids 38

Eappen, Matthew 110
Edward III 6
Edward IV 6, 7
egg poachers 120
Elizabeth I 8, 9, 10
Elizabeth II 115, 117
English Civil War 16
Evans, Chris 83, 84, 117–9

Featherstonehaugh, Sir
    Harry 18
Fitton, Lady 10
Fitton, Mary 8–11, 90
Fitton, Sir Edward 8
flogging 28
Fordham, Peta 45, 46

Gallows Hill, Boughton 22
Gawsworth Hall 8, 9, 11
gibbeting 22, 24, 25
Girls Aloud 98, 99, 100
Grace, W.G. 41
Great Train Robbery 44–6
Greville, Charles 18, 19
Grundy, Bill 50, 51
Gun Hill 24

Hamilton, Christine 67, 70,
    92–4
Hamilton, Col John 12, 13
Hamilton, Duke of 12, 13
Hamilton, Lady Emma
    18–20
Hamilton, Neil 67, 69, 70,
    80, 92–4, 112–4
Hamilton, Sir William 19,
    20
hamster-eating 83
hanging 22, 24
Harding, Sarah 98, 99
Harry, Prince 114, 115,
    117
Hawke, Lord 41
Henry VIII, 7
Herbert, William, Earl of
    Pembroke 9, 10
Higgins, Edward 73–6
Hindley, Myra 32
Hornby, Albert Neilson
    39–43
Howard, Michael 97
Hughes, William Thomas
    52–5

*I'm a Celebrity Get Me Out
    of Here* 51, 94, 117
IRA 59–63, 106
'Itsy Bitsy Teeny Weeny' 82

Jack the Ripper 124–8
Johnson, Hewlet 81
Johnston, Brian 58–9
Jones, Poll 90
Joy Division 56

Kemp, William 10, 11
Kenyon, Peter 84
King's School, Macclesfield 14, 56, 81
Klosowski, Lucy 124, 128
Klosowski, Severin 124, 128
Knollys, Sir Robert 6
Knollys, Sir William 8, 10
Knutsford County Gaol 27, 28
Knutsford Heath 67, 69, 70, 74–6

Lancashire County Cricket Club 39
Leigh, Sir Piers 7
Light Brigade, Charge of 18
Lindow Moss, bog man 36–8
'Love Will Tear Us Apart' 56
Lyon, Amy 18

Maccartney, George 12, 13
Macclesfield
  Parish Church 7
  West Park Museum 78, 79
Mallet, Timothy 82
Malloy, Bryan 24
Manchester Airport disaster 57, 58
Manchester United Football Club 84
Marsh, George 22, 23
Maxwell, Robert 104
Methane, Mr 87–9
Mills, Jack 44–6
Mohun, Lord 12, 13

Moran, Gill 52, 53, 55
Moran, Richard 52, 53, 55
Mother Redcap 90, 91
Mouldsworth murders 128–9

Nabarro, Sir Gerald 94
Nantwich 16, 40–3
Naples 19, 20
Neil, Det Supt Arthur Fowler 124, 127
Nelson, Fanny (Nisbet) 20
Nelson, Horatia 20
Nelson, Admiral Horatio Lord 18–20
Northgate Gaol 24, 27

Oake, Det Cons Stephen 71
Oakes, Wallace Arnold 46–7
O'Connor, Des 83
Onassis, Tina 104

panda, giant 78, 79
Parker, Lord Chief Justice 13
parish constables 22
Potter, Lynda Lee 95
Pottery Cottage murders 52, 53
pressing, death by 22
Prestbury bank murders 130–2
Priest, Nicola 60
prisoners' rebellion 29
Pulford murder 27

Rainow 51–5
Richard III 6, 7
Risley, HM Prison 28–30
Romans 1
Rossiter, Mark 60
Rotten, Johnny 50, 51
Royal Society for Protection of Birds 120

Royal Ulster Constabulary 106, 107, 110

Secret Policeman, The 33, 34
Sex Pistols 50, 51
Shaa, Sir Edmund 6
Shaa, Dr Ralph 6
Shakespeare, William 8, 10
Shipman, Dr Harold 133–6
Smith, Ian Duncan 96
Smith, Trumpet Maj William 18
smuggling 90, 91
Spencer, Lady Diana 114
squirrels, 76–8
Stalker, John 106–10
Starchaser Industries Ltd 86
Starr, Freddie 82, 83
Stockport air crash 47–9
stocks, 21, 22
Styal, HM Prison 28–9, 30–2
SWAT squad 71, 72

Taylor, Elizabeth (Bessie) 125, 126, 127, 128
Taylor, Kevin 107
Test Match, 1991 58, 59
Tyburn 15
Tyler, Wat 6

Virgin Radio 118, 119

Waite, Terry 120, 121
Warrington
  Bridge Street 60, 61, 66
  Museum 24, 25, 26
  Peace Centre 61
Warrington Guardian 60–3, 127
Whitehouse, Mary 92
William, Prince 114, 115, 117
Winterton, Lady Ann 95–7
Woodward, Louise 110, 111